ECONOMICS
PRIMER

ECONOMICS PRIMER

Linda Low
Singapore University of Social Sciences, Singapore

World Scientific

EW JERSEY · LONDON · SINGAPORE · BEIJING · SHANGHAI · HONG KONG · TAIPEI · CHENNAI · TOKYO

Published by

World Scientific Publishing Co. Pte. Ltd.

5 Toh Tuck Link, Singapore 596224

USA office: 27 Warren Street, Suite 401-402, Hackensack, NJ 07601

UK office: 57 Shelton Street, Covent Garden, London WC2H 9HE

National Library Board, Singapore Cataloguing in Publication Data
Name: Low, Linda.
Title: Economics primer / Linda Low.
Description: Singapore : World Scientific, [2020]
Identifier(s): OCN 1140677714 | ISBN 978-981-12-1843-9 (paperback) |
    ISBN 978-981-12-1792-0 (hardcover)
Subject: LCSH: Economics.
Classification: DDC 330--dc23

British Library Cataloguing-in-Publication Data
A catalogue record for this book is available from the British Library.

For any available supplementary material, please visit
https://www.worldscientific.com/worldscibooks/10.1142/11764#t=suppl

Desk Editor: Jiang Yulin

Typeset by Stallion Press
Email: enquiries@stallionpress.com

Printed in Singapore

This Primer is for Maddy

About the Author

Linda Low, Associate Professor, Singapore University of Social Sciences, started in the Ministry of Finance, Singapore doing tax research before joining the National University of Singapore, then became a Senior Research Fellow at the Institute of Southeast Asian Studies (now Yusof Ishak Institute, Singapore). For eight years, she was the Head of Strategic Planning in Abu Dhabi Government (United Arab Emirates, UAE) and Senior Economic Adviser for Abu Dhabi Council for Economic Development as well as Adjunct Professor at UAE University and UAE Higher Colleges for Technology. Her research includes public sector economics and public policy, public enterprises and privatisation, social security and retirement, ageing, health economics, human resources development and manpower policies, international trade and regionalism, international political economy and development economics, with publications in Asia-Pacific, Association of Southeast Asian Nations (ASEAN) and Gulf Cooperation Council (GCC). She works with the Asia-Pacific Economic Cooperation (APEC) and Asia-Pacific Economic Cooperation Council (PECC). She also collaborates with National Trades Union Congress (NTUC) and Singapore Civil Service College for skills training.

Contents

Chapter 1
Introduction

Introduction

Quoting a poem by Rudyard Kipling, this Primer has the same aims as his six honest serving men:

> I keep six honest serving-men
> (They taught me all I knew);
> Their names are What and Why and When
> And How and Where and Who.

This Primer is preparatory Economics, simplified for students and laymen in daily life, as a stepping stone to understand more complex economic events around the world today. This chapter reviews some basic economic concepts as a start.

Circular flow

In an integrated globalised world economy, there is nowhere to hide in economies open to trade, investment and people crossing borders. Figure 1.1 shows the circular flow among the main economic actors as households and firms. They represent demand and supply respectively with government in taxation and expenditure. Adding trade makes an open economy with foreign households, firms and governments in action.

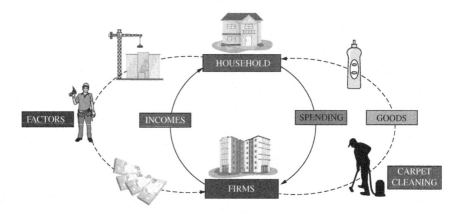

Figure 1.1   Circular flow

The factors comprise land, labour and capital, used by firms to produce goods and services, demanded by households also as suppliers of labour. Economics is about human behaviour making rational decisions in consumption, saving, production and investment, all grounded on benefits and costs or net benefits.

In circular flow models, the basic actors in any economy are the consumers in households on the demand side and producers in businesses or firms on the supply side to reflect the see-saw in Figure 1.2. The same in a basic circular flow in Figure 1.8 shows businesses produce and supply goods and services to the households. Households in turn provide factors of production in land, labour and capital.

Closed and open economies

Starting as a closed economy, Figure 1.2 shows a see-saw definition of unlimited human wants (heavy end) in contrast to limited resources (lighter end) with the balancing by the private and/or public (government) sectors.

Figure 1.2 as a see-saw definition of economics is appropriate as economics is about an optimum balancing of scarcity of resources as factors of production or inputs to maximize production commodities as

See-saw definition: economic trade-off & opportunity cost (3 questions of what, how & for whom)

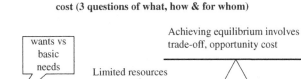

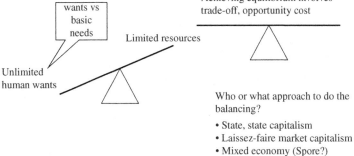

Figure 1.2   See-saw definition of economics

goods and services or outputs as unlimited human wants. Human satisfaction is beyond basic needs in food, clothing and shelter to become luxury goods.

Understanding that economic growth is quantitative as gross domestic product (GDP) and economic development is quality of life. More consumption of goods and services is desired to attain social welfare which is based on some distribution systems by the government. Individuals and households make rational choices for private goods. The government's collective role in defence and police is rational. It is rational in providing public education and public health for society as a whole based on externalities of public goods. Singapore excels as its competitive advantage lies in its human resource development.

The circular flow concept in Figure 1.3 shows what goes around, comes around. The inner set of arrows show a barter exchange of goods and services. In a monetised economy, money is a medium of exchange. The outer set of arrows show consumer spending paid to businesses which in turn pay households factor incomes in wages and earnings.

To illustrate the basic circular flow, Figure 1.3 is a simple closed economy of domestic households and firms. There is no international trade, government and other intermediaries like financial institutions as

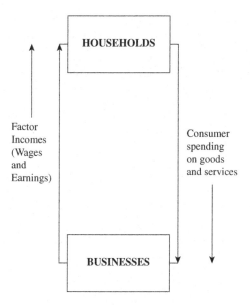

Figure 1.3   The basic circular flow model

banks, equity and capital market or labour market. Circular flows are self-equilibrating without any intervention or intermediation.

Figure 1.4 shows a more realistic circular flow of income and spending in an open economy. It incorporates other economic agents, mainly, government, rest of the world or world economy with exports and imports, and financial markets as intermediaries for saving and investment. In an open economy, foreign households and businesses are at work in all transactions.

Distinguishing the flows further into leakages and injections:

- Injections are flows which increase circular flows and economic activity as a whole. They comprise investment (I) to increase production capacity, export (X) to earn foreign exchange from the rest of the world and government spending (G) of state provided goods and services.
- Leakages are the contra flows as they decrease circular flows. They are the reverse of injections in terms of saving (S), import (M) and taxation (T).

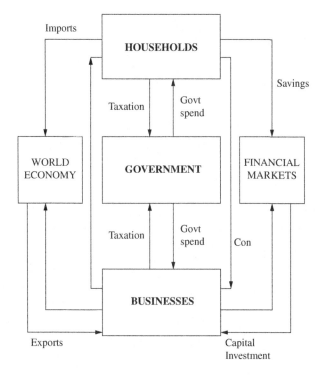

Figure 1.4   Income and spending flows

The resulting identities of I = S, X = M and G = T imply public policies can fine-tune these variables, help to stabilize and manage the economy. A shock into the system from domestic or external forces disturbs
any prior equilibrium. An understanding of the interrelationships among
all the variables including their nature and scope of influence is vital for
all economic actors to play their part in the economy.

Figure 1.5 on structure of economics brings out more concepts and
methodology. Flows and stocks of goods are clear with households
and firms in microeconomics and macroeconomics including government
and rest of the world.

Laws of demand and supply determining equilibrium price and quantity, movement and shift of demand and supply curves, and concepts of
elasticity serve both production and consumer theories.

Demand
• Price of good/service
• Prices of other good/service
• Income
• Tastes
• Population (size, demography)
• Others (government policy, etc)

Supply
• Price of good/service
• Prices of factors of production (land, labour, capital)
• Number of sellers
• Technology, know-how
• Government policy, regulation

Figure 1.5   Determinants of demand and supply

Laws of demand and supply

Consumers and producers respond to mainly to price in their respective laws of demand and supply. Consumers prefer lower prices to consume more as inversely related, downward-sloping demand curve. Producers are for higher prices with upward-sloping supply curve. Their determinants are in Figure 1.5.

Price is the independent (endogenous) factor determining demand and supply with all other dependent factors (exogenous) held constant (*ceteris paribus*). Figure 1.6 shows demand and supply intersecting in equilibrium with market-clearing price (p) and quantity (q) and their corresponding demand and supply equations.

Movement and shift

For both demand and supply, change in price results in movement along their respective curves with corresponding change in quantity. Distinguished from movement, shift of demand and supply curves means factors other than price change or a relaxation of *ceteris paribus* assumption. Parallel shifts reflect *ceteris paribus* as constant for all other determinants.

Figures 1.7 and 1.8 show respectively, a shift of a demand and a supply curve responding to a change an exogenous factor. Demand shifts outward (inward) with a rise (fall) in income. The parallel shift reflects *ceteris paribus* still held for other determinants. Supply shifts outward (inward) with a rise (fall) in technology.

In both cases, an outward shift of a curve denotes an increase in quantity demanded as rising income enables more demand or more supplied with lower labour. Conversely, an inward shift is a decrease in quantity demanded or supplied due to falling income or rising labour costs, respectively.

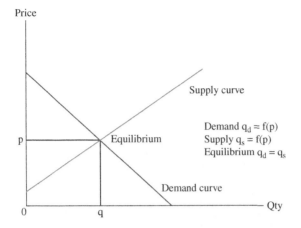

Figure 1.6 Demand–supply equilibrium

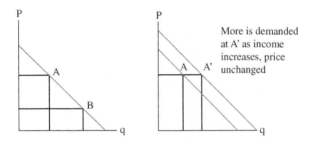

Figure 1.7 Shift of demand curve

In the real world, movements and shifts of both demand and supply curves can occur simultaneously and iteratively in Figures 1.7 and 1.8, respectively. Market equilibrium adjusts to both endogenous and exogenous factors, with or without government intervention. Some final equilibrium settles until another disturbance or shock to the system stops.

Elasticity

Elasticity measures the responsiveness of one variable (like quantity demanded or supplied) in response to another variable (price). Basic staple goods like rice are demand inelastic while luxuries like vacations are elastics or more sensitive to price. For demand, a simple algebraic

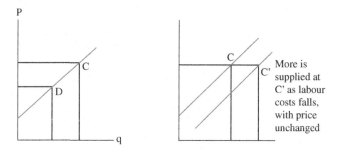

Figure 1.8   Shift of supply curve

measure of responsiveness is the percentage change in quantity demanded to percentage change in price, as:

Price elasticity of demand = – (% change in quantity demanded) / (% change in price)

The negative sign for price elasticity of demand reflects the law of demand in the negative correlation of quantity and price. When price increases, quantity falls and when price falls, quantity increases for normal goods.

The determinants of price elasticity of demand are:

- Availability of substitutes; more substitutes, more price elastic as different types of food, but education and health services are relatively price inelastic
- Time factor allowing taste to adjust to price changes

The slopes of demand and supply curves matter. A flatter slope and a steeper slope denote elastic and inelastic demand and supply, respectively. In Figure 1.9, an extreme case of a vertical supply curve is inelastic land in Singapore in contrast to air as perfectively elastic in being available.

Cross price elasticity

Cross price elasticity of demand measures how demand of one good reacts to changes in the price of other goods.

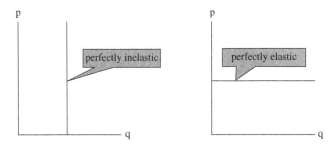

Figure 1.9 Extreme elasticity cases

Cross price elasticity = – (% change in quantity of one good) /
(% change in price of another good)

A positive sign for cross price elasticity of demand indicates that the goods are substitutes. It is negative when the goods are complements.

Income elasticity

The concept of income elasticity shows the impact of income beside changes in the prices of other goods on quantity demanded. Income elasticity of demand measures how demand reacts to changes in income.

Income elasticity of demand = % change in quantity demanded /
% change in income

The result is positive for a normal good, that is, it obeys the law of demand. If it is negative, the good is inferior as in the case of rice. As income rises, we eat less rice as meat and fish become affordable. Generally, normal goods are income elastic, luxuries have income elasticities greater than unity and inferior goods have negative income elasticities.

Structure of economics

As shown in Figure 1.10, economics can be qualitatively and quantitatively studied.

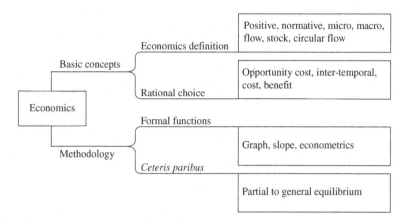

Figure 1.10   Structure of economics

Opportunity cost and trade-off are costs and benefits rationally weighed or as net. More considerations in choices are inter-temporal involving time as current, future and even inter-generational as well as cyclical short-run and long-run structural issues.

While economics is a social science, scientific methods and mathematical tools study universal economic laws of "what is" as descriptive and generalised positive economics. Human economic behaviour, however rational or irrational, means a normative prescriptive side as "what it should be" as more varied in different economic and political systems.

Econometrics is a study of economics with mathematics, involving big data as analytics to complex models for forecasting. The cause and effect of one factor as price on quantity demanded by one household is partial equilibrium to derive the law of demand for all households in general equilibrium.

Quintessentially, economics as households and firms or consumer and production theories respectively in Figure 1.11 is microeconomics.

Chapter 8 depicts Macroeconomics with government and trade sectors.

Figure 1.12 shows how hypothesis with assumptions graduates into an econometric model. Empirical evidence, data and information test and verify the model systematically. It becomes a law like the laws of demand

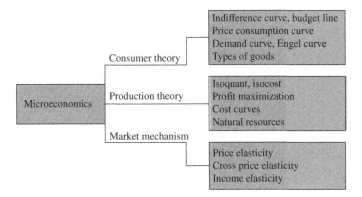

Figure 1.11   Microeconomics

Modeling: hypothesis & law

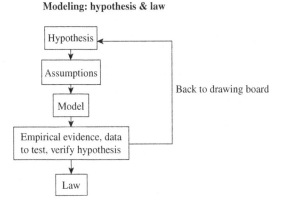

Figure 1.12   From hypothesis to law

and supply. These apply universally for all prices and quantities in demand and supply.

Real world

Basic tools in economics in theory as applied and viewed in the real world are complicated by politics, geography, history, culture and a myriad of other factors. See Figure 1.13 as encompassing all these. This complexity requires a more multidisciplinary approach.

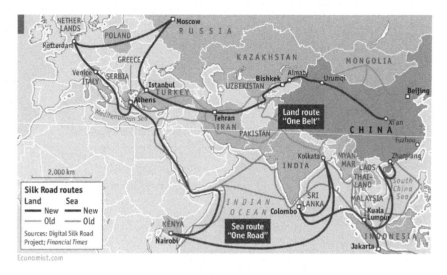

Figure 1.13   One-Belt-One-Road, BRI, AIIB

Recommended videos and Chapter 9 show the realities of geoeconomics and geopolitics:

Global Financial Crisis	https://www.youtube.com/watch?v= N9YLta5Tr2A
Euro crisis	https://www.youtube.com/watch?v= j4_tyEl84IQ
One Belt, One Road (OBOR)	https://www.youtube.com/watch?v= V_bfM_aT1Yk&t=

Structure of book

Rather than describe the content of the following eight chapters of the Primer, each of the following figures may capture the essence more simplistically.

Chapter 2 Production Theory

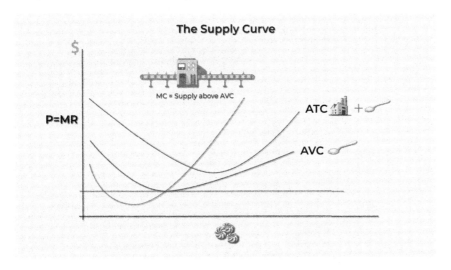

Chapter 3 Market Structure

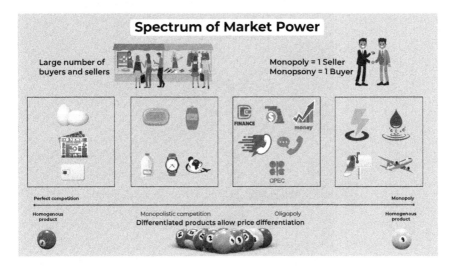

Chapter 4   Consumer Theory

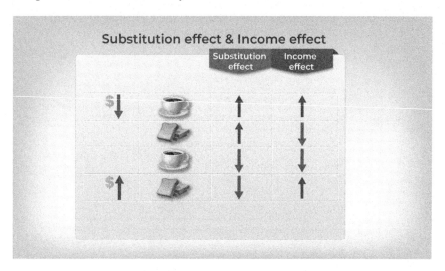

Chapter 5   Labour Market

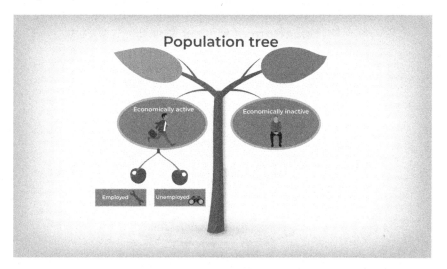

Chapter 6   Government

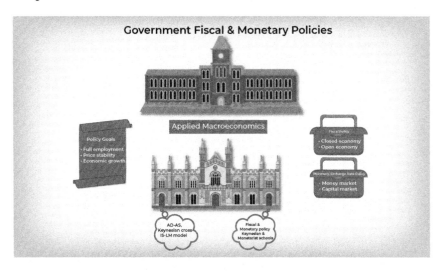

Chapter 7   International Economy

Trade liberalisation: tariff, NTBs

• Unilateral (national)

• FTA (bilateral)

• Regional (RTA, ASEAN, EU)
  – Preferential trading area
    step-by-step cuts tariff
  – Free trade area (AFTA)
  – Customs union
  – Single market
  – Monetary union (€zone)

• Multilateral (WTO)
  – GTA/WTO consistent
  – MFN, market access,
    national treatment

Chapter 8   Macroeconomics

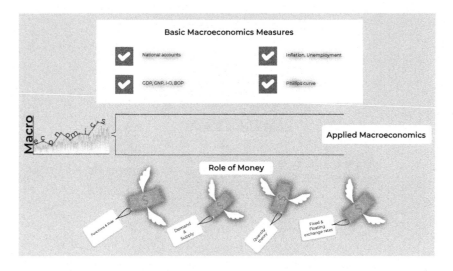

Chapter 9   Geoeconomics, Geopolitics

This Time is Different: A Panaroramic View of Eight Centuries of Financial Crises. Carmen M M. **Reinhart** & Kenneth S. **Rogoff**, 2009, 2014, Princeton University Press

Crisis of Credit Visualised: http://crisisofcredit.com/

or

https://youtube.com/watch?v=bxLWm6_6ta

Chapter 2

Production Theory

Introduction

From macroeconomic at the top, aggregate production in an economy simplified to two goods in Figure 2.1 as the production possibility curve. Given limited resources, the economy can produce guns or butter (food) along the production possibility curve with B as more guns or C as more food. Outputs at A are suboptimal, that is, underutilised resources not maximising production. Outputs at X are unattainable unless the production possibility curve can shift outward by more resources or with technology improving productivity.

At the microeconomic level, applying production theory examines revenue, cost and profit for different market structures in Chapter 3. Concepts include isoquant, isocost, producer equilibrium, cost curves, output decision, market supply among others.

Production theory

The producer decides:

- What to produce?
- How to produce in choice of production function as combinations of factors of production as capital and labour to demand/employ in production?
- For whom to produce?

17

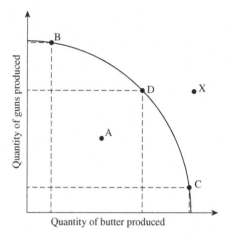

Figure 2.1   Production possibility curve

The producer or entrepreneur organises land, labour and capital (with embodied technology) as inputs to produce output of goods and services for a profit. It may equally be from a family-owned business or a state-owned enterprise (SOE) or government-linked company (GLC) in Singapore. The company can operate at home and abroad.

In microeconomics, with land deemed invariable as a country's natural endowment, a two-factor total product or production function in Figure 2.2 depicts a level of output produced (Qs) in a technologically-determined process with capital (K) held constant and labour (L) variable, or Qs = f(K, L).

In production theory, the short-run is defined as a time horizon when at least one factor of production is held constant, usually K. In the long-run, nothing is fixed or constant. All factors are variable, including technology to in turn enable or affect renewable resources. Accordingly, different time horizons have production and output decisions taken.

Two features are implicit in the production function. One is its shape. As more and more of variable L is used, total output increases, but at a decreasing rate until reaching a peak. Thereafter, the law of diminishing returns to the variable factor sets in with output falling.

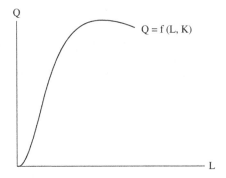

Figure 2.2 Production function

With more resources and technology, the production function can be lifted up in the long run. Fixed variable K increases with capital accumulation wisely invested or a higher level of technology increases labour productivity with automation and new skills.

Technology is the key to productivity for both K and L. It lowers costs, thus inflation too. Achieving higher productivity is either by less inputs used for the same output or the same inputs producing a higher output. An educated and trained workforce enabled or associated with technology either reduces manpower used for the same output or the same manpower producing more. This is productivity as consciously honed by policy.

A second feature of the production function is it solves the engineering and managerial aspects of technical efficiency. The firm in microeconomics focuses on allocative efficiency to make allocative choices of how much of each input factor to use, given factor prices and technology determined by the production function.

The decision frame in the short-run has one or more inputs held constant, namely, K and L is variable. In the long-run, both K and L factors are variable, that is, the firm can expand, but the production function itself remains fixed. In the very long-run, with a choice in technology possible, the firm may even have a choice of various possible production functions, as in more capital-intensive, less labour-intensive for Singapore.

The production function relates physical inputs to physical outputs. Prices and costs are implicit in allocative efficiency. The distinction between returns to scale (inputs to output) and economies of scale (input costs to output) is where cost functions are more explicit as noted later.

Isoquant

The microeconomics of consumer theory (Chapter 4) of indifference curves and budget lines have in parallel their counterparts in production theory in isoquants and isocosts, respectively. The law of diminishing marginal utility in consumption is akin to the law of diminishing marginal returns to a factor in production in the short-run.

Figure 2.3 shows an isoquant where the producer is indifferent to C or D. Both produce the same output level using different factor combinations. A certain state of technology or a given production function is assumed for a mapping of isoquants, each representing a different quantity of output.

Isoquants are typically convex to the origin to reflect the two factors are substitutable for each other at varying rates. Isoquants are L-shaped for two inputs as perfect substitutes. The marginal rate of technical substitution (MRTS) is the slope at a point as negative for substitution. The MRTS is the change in one input (delta K) per unit change in the other input (delta L) that is just sufficient to maintain a constant level of production.

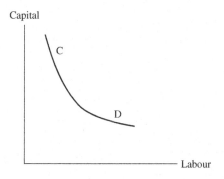

Figure 2.3   Isoquant

$$MRTS = - (\Delta K/\Delta L)$$

An isoquant map can indicate returns to scale by the spacing or distance of isoquants:

- Equal distances mean constant returns to scale, the same ratio for inputs to output.
- For increasing returns to scale, distances between the isoquants on the map decrease. Attaining the next level of higher output is with a smaller proportionate rise of inputs. A doubling of inputs will result more than double of output, so the isoquant shifts outward with the distance decreased.
- For decreasing returns to scale, distances between the isoquants on the map increase. As output increases, as in the firm's production function doubling inputs, it will result in an isoquant placed proportionately further away from the previous isoquant.

Typically, a firm has decreasing, constant then increasing returns to scale reflected in increasing, constant and decreasing distances between the isoquants on the map. Once the law of diminishing marginal returns to a fixed factor sets in, decreasing returns to scale occurs in the short-run. In the long-run, with no factor assumed fixed, the law does not apply.

Isocost

As a budget line, a firm faces an isocost in Figure 2.4. Total cost (TC) is the sum of all factor costs, that is, K (all non-human factors of production with interest rate r as the rental price) and L priced as wage (w). The slope of the isocost is the relative price of the factors of production or $-$ (w/r), the negative sign denoting a downward-sloping line.

$$TC = rK + wL$$

$$K = - (w/r)L + TC/r$$

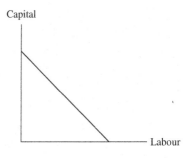

Figure 2.4   Isocost

Producer equilibrium

Bringing together Figures 2.3 and 2.4, a producer equilibrium at E is a technical optimum in Figure 2.5. It optimizes the isocost as well in a tangency between an isoquant and an isocost:

$$MRTS = -(\Delta K/\Delta L) = -(w/r)$$

In theory, E is also a profit maximization point, with technical and allocative efficiency attained. The maximization condition of MC = MR will be explored with cost curves more fully considered.

Profit maximisation occurs when MR (addition to revenue from sale of one more unit of product) is equal to MC (addition to cost from production of one more unit of product). Other objectives may include sales maximisation, business or corporate growth and diversification. Market entry into a foreign economy has many more challenges.

Cost curves

The isocost as TC can be broken down into total fixed cost (TFC) or sunk cost as invariant to quantity produced, always incurred even when not in production plus total variable cost (TVC) in the short-run as shown in Figure 2.6 for cost versus quantity.

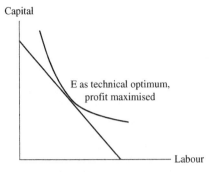

Figure 2.5   Production equilibrium

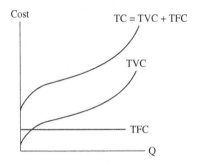

Figure 2.6   Total cost curves

Figure 2.7 translates the information into the supply curve (P versus Q) with average cost curves derived as:

$$AC = TC/q$$

$$AFC = TFC/q$$

$$AVC = TVC/q$$

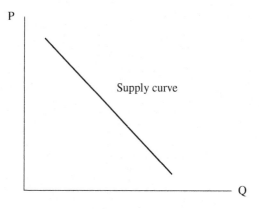

Figure 2.7   The supply curve (I)

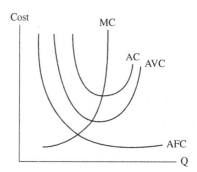

Figure 2.8   Average, marginal cost curves

Whereas TFC is a flat horizontal line in Figure 2.6, AFC declines with more units produced to cover the sunk cost, before flattening to a constant in Figure 2.8.

Marginal cost (MC) is the increment in TC with the last unit produced or:

$$MC = \Delta TC / \Delta q$$

MC curve passes through the minimum points of ATC and AVC curves in Figure 2.9 to be the supply curve too, that is, MC = supply curve above AVC.

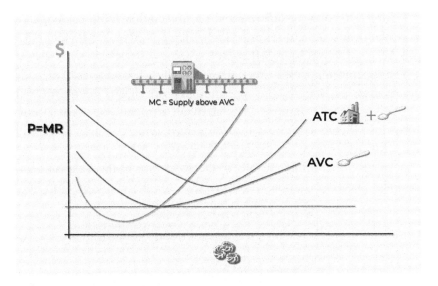

Figure 2.9   The supply curve (II)

Output decision

Profit defined as TC less total revenue (TR) and TR is a product of price and quantity sold or:

$$TR = pq$$

$$MR = \Delta TR/\Delta q = price$$

MR is the increment in revenue with each unit produced. Assuming a firm is a price-taker, a relatively small component in the market with no market power in a competitive market, MR = price.

In theory, the firm makes profit as long as price covers AC, or at least AVC or MR > MC. The firm continues to expand output until the profit maximisation condition MC = MR is reached. It means the cost of the last unit produced is equal to its revenue when sold, a breakeven concept. The price-taking profit-maximising firm sets price as:

$$p^* = MR = MC$$

Figure 2.10 shows a supernormal profit situation. With some market power, the firm is able to set price higher than p*, that is, MR more than cover AC or MR > AC and MR > MC.

The supernormal profit situation may not last. If competition prevails, entry of firms attracted by the supernormal profit means more firms will increase supply and dampen price until all earn only a normal profit as shown in Figure 2.11. This is also deemed zero economic profit with price = MC to cover AC or defined as p = MC = AC.

A supernormal profit prevails in the short-run. In the long-run, zero economic profit or normal profit is due to the entry of firm in a

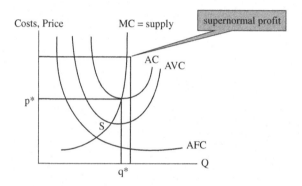

Figure 2.10   Supernormal profit

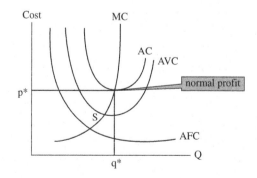

Figure 2.11   Normal profit

competitive market. It means no entry and no exit as existing firms earn just enough to stay, that is, opportunity cost of not exiting is sufficiently compensated.

After normal profit, the price is between two critical points. Figure 2.12 has several features for the firm's decision:

- Price can fall below AC, but still above AVC denoting respectively, a sub-normal profit and a shutdown point S.
- The firm may not shut down yet as long as price = MC covers AVC.
- Below S, the firm has no reason to exist.
- This makes the portion of MC above S the supply curve. Prices on MC above S show viable sub-normal profit progressing to normal and supernormal up the MC.

In summary, Table 2.1 shows the firm's output decisions as:

Table 2.1   Firm's output decisions

Profit	Price
Supernormal profit	p = MR > AC, MR > MC
Normal, zero economic profit	p = MR = AC, MR = MC
Sub-normal	p = MR < AC, MR < MC
Shutdown	p = MR < AVC, MR < MC

With costs considered, Table 2.2 shows the relationship between returns to scale (physical inputs to output) and economies of scale (input costs to output) using long-run AC curve (LRAC) in Figure 2.13. Both concepts are depicted on the same LRAC as physical inputs variable in the long-run translates to AC. Assume a doubling of inputs:

- Increasing returns to scale means more than double output, equivalent to economies of scale or decreasing cost.
- Constant returns to scale means double output to attain constant cost.
- Decreasing returns to scale means less than double output or diseconomies or increasing cost.

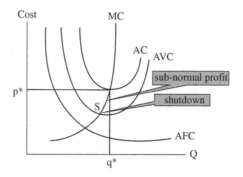

Figure 2.12   Sub-normal profit and shutdown

Table 2.2   Relationship between returns to scale and economies of scale

Returns to scale: input to output	Economies of scale: input cost to output	Assume double inputs
Decreasing returns	Increasing cost (diseconomies)	Less than double output
Constant returns	Constant cost	Double output
Increasing returns	Decreasing cost (economies)	More than double output

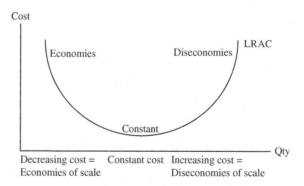

Figure 2.13   Economies of scale

In reality, no firm would operate with increasing cost or rising LRAC. The LRAC is usually only L-shaped with only economies of scale enjoyed until constant cost sets in.

Market supply

The portion of MC above shutdown point S is the supply curve. This is derived by horizontally summing a number of firms' supply curves to yield the market supply curve in Figure 2.14.

Bringing in both market demand and market supply, their intersection yields an equilibrium. From time to time, an equilibrium may be disturbed. An excess demand as in Figure 2.15 may be due to a higher seasonal demand like Christmas. An excess supply in Figure 2.16 occurs with a bumper crop of nuts, for instance.

The price mechanism or "invisible hand" will be in motion to self-correct these excesses. Sometimes, the needed information enables the market forces of demand and supply to attain equilibrium again. Information on prices, alternative sources of supply or

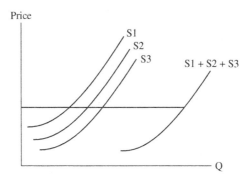

Figure 2.14   Market supply

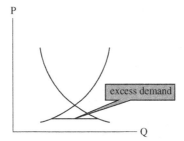

Figure 2.15   Excess demand

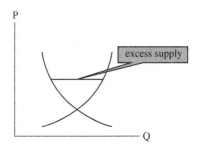

Figure 2.16   Excess supply

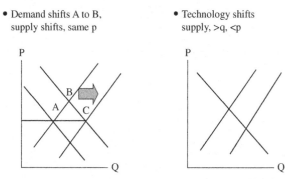

Figure 2.17   Adjusting equilibrium

consumers shopping more wisely if not postponing demand may work. Otherwise, the government may step in to help the market mechanism adjust.

So as not to interfere with market forces, caution is for government price control as market knows best in lasseiz-faire. A more careful economic analysis of the causes and reasons for market disequilibrium may suggest less drastic measures. Both the government and responsible suppliers may increase supply of goods during festive seasons to satisfy demand, provide more price information, available with price monitoring for consumer education.

Figure 2.17 shows two forms of market adjustment. When demand moves from A to B on the left-hand side, price increases until supply shifts in response to bring price back to the original level. Technology on the right-hand side means expansion in capacity, leads to an increase in supply to shift right. A higher supply with lower price is beneficial to all.

Generally, the government intervenes only as a last resort, especially through laws and regulations. The economics of a minimum wage in Chapter 5 or a tariff in imports in Chapter 7 will show their respective market distortions as "neutral" policy intervention is difficult. More government market-supporting measures should suffice.

Natural resources, renewable and non-renewable

Singapore is small, resource-lacking together with scarcity of labour amid an ageing demography. Augmented by foreign labour, both skilled and especially in other manual work, emphasis on human resources development and management at all levels accompanies capital-intensive production. Renewable as solar energy is a potential, with NEWater as recycled water being a tapping technology as well as water-saving ways and habits.

The Report of the Committee on the Future Economy (CFE), in a word, sees the future as digital, harnessing information and communications technology (ICT) more intensely. Unsurprisingly, the Singapore economy is more service-oriented and based on finance, transportation, tourism, education, health and other management services in accounting, legal and ICT. Singapore's location and good governance make it a hub or regional capital for other foreign multinational companies (MNCs).

Inter-temporal choice

Inter-temporal choices apply to the microeconomics of consumers and firms. Time affects elasticity concepts with respect to demand, supply and income. Household spending or saving as postponed consumption, in bank deposits also serves as funds for investment as firms borrowing, in turn affecting the supply for firms (circular flow in Chapter 1).

Firms have time horizons to plan the transition from short-run to long-run with technical, cost or allocative efficiency. For firms, maximising profit remains the ultimate goal among others. The right time for each objective needs the right pricing strategies in four generic forms: marginal cost pricing, incremental pricing, break even pricing and mark-up pricing. Pricing strategies are usually integrated into a wider mix of factors other than price.

These include product characteristics and consumer perception of them, distribution channels and promotion as effective marketing, credit provision and advertisement as well as product cycle in Figure 2.18.

Prudent government planning with policies fine-tuned to strategies in a quintessentially market economy works as another effective intertemporal choice. As the CFE prepares for a digital future, the right manpower policy with rewiring and rehiring, not retiring (Figure 2.19 offers three books) is to ensure employability given ageing labour demography and not over relying on foreign labour.

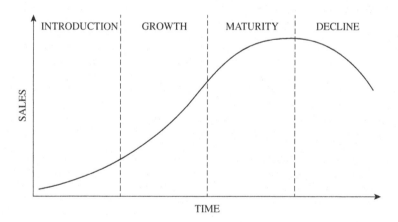

Figure 2.18   Product lifecycle

Robert K Critchley: 3 Books

2002
Rewired, Rehired
or Retired? A
Global Guide for
the Experienced
Worker?

2004
Doing Nothing is
Not an Option!
Facing the
Imminent
Labor Crisis

2006
Rewire or Rust!

Figure 2.19 Books from Robert K. Critchley

Chapter 3
Market Structure

Introduction

This chapter will discuss four market structures as perfect, monopolistic, oligopoly and monopoly to see how each attains profit maximisation by their respective pricing strategies. The law of diminishing returns and concepts as returns to scale, economies of scale (noted in Chapter 2) and economies of scope under respective market structures will also be analysed.

Competition spectrum

Producers or markets on the supply side for goods and services are organised in four structures as shown in Figure 3.1. They differ mainly in number of sellers, ease of entry and differentiation in product as similar/homogeneous or otherwise. Government and public policy also affect the degree of competition depending on the sector and economy.

A quick revision in terminology is products denoting both goods and services. Many firms in similar products form an industry or sector. It can be private sector for profit maximisation or public sector involving governments for essential products like for public utilities.

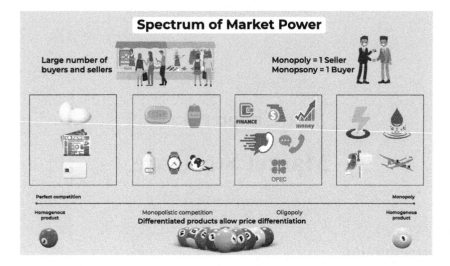

Figure 3.1   Competitive spectrum: From perfect competition to monopoly

Perfect competition

Perfect competition seems to be a textbook case as in stock markets with many stockbrokers. All corporate shares are listed at the same prices and buyers are free to choose stockbrokers. It is the same in any hawker centre for coffee or tea or a quick simple lunch if workers go nearby for time and travel conveniences. Information is perfect too with no product preferences or producers making prices with cost or other advantages. Profit-making is the main objective for perfect competition.

Many buyers and sellers for identical products face free entry and exit as conditions for sustained competition. The result means firms are price-takers as the industry as a whole sets prices. The resultant equilibrium in perfect competition is when existing firms stay and no new firms enter. All earn normal profits with no exit or existing firms earn enough to stay as well as no entry, with no supernormal profit to attract new firms in the long run.

Monopolistic competition

Branding for instance can have consumer products in clothing or food and drinks become more differentiated. Beverages like Coke, Pepsi,

Sarsaparilla, root beer or local flavours as chrysanthemum or restaurants rated by Michelin series, move them into a monopolistic range. Customer loyalty with awards also plays a part in competition, same as certain specialists in hospitals for maternity or children.

Monopolistic competition becomes less perfect as differentiated products, even as close substitutes as shampoos or soaps as special formulae. Advertisement adds to the differences with prices varying accordingly. Consumers remain free to make their choices while advertising can be as informative as persuasive even with film stars endorsing certain products as advertising or gamic. Profit-making remains the main objective for monopolistic competition.

Oligopoly

In the real world, oligopoly is the most common market structure for products with high capital and technology requirements. One is where costs are usually high with high capital and equipment needed and other features. Only a few producers make the products to operate as an oligopoly. Industries making automobiles and airplanes or even running airlines are typically oligopolies. With few producers, they have market power in making prices, but buyers still have choices between a Toyota touted as fuel-efficient as Japan is an oil importer or bigger American cars if gasoline from America is not as much a concern.

Airlines specialise more in services, same as telecommunication companies as non-price competition. After sales service may also count in competition, same as airlines and hotels partnerships tie up as more oligopolistic. For ease and efficiency as sending and picking passengers to hotels by airlines, such business partnerships may also suit the average cost-conscious travellers, all with awards or points to earn. It works like frequent-flyer programmes to gain mileage under similar point systems as marketing as non-price competition.

In oil, oil producers in the Middle East as endowed by natural geography have formed the Organization of the Petroleum Exporting Countries (OPEC), but OPEC membership has variously Indonesia and other African and South American states with Qatar possibly opting out. As a carter, OPEC members control supply (based on respective members' historic output) which in turn "sets" prices as a cartel. Cartels as few sellers in collusion in quotas or pricing or both also engender cheating by members. As OPEC members grew even outside of traditional trusted Arabic members, their oligopolistic power fall in commensurate.

As OPEC shows, game theory in economics becomes relevant in considering the interactions and behaviours among all participants as producers and consumers using mathematical models of strategic interaction of such rational decision-makers. Game theory applied to oligopolistic markets studies all behavioural moves both as profitable or best strategies. The decision-makers as producers and buyers are players in the game as pay-offs for certain outcomes. With Saudi Arabia's dominance in OPEC, it exercises some form of price leadership, but cheating is as troublesome as an inducement by others too to go below the OPEC price to sell more as revenue too. Such collusive price leadership by OPEC does require a lot of like-minded collusion with cheating as deviant behaviour to be penalised.

Apart from cheating, such "unfair" competition as high prices by oil cartels has further motivated substitutes as renewables. Solar, wind and water for energy are as renewable as they are effective substitutes with the support by states as energy is key for industry and security of nations. The International Atomic Energy Agency (IAEA) controls nuclear power for military use since 1957. As an oil importer, despite nuclear bombs dropped in Hiroshima and Nagasaki in 1945 during World War II by the US as an allied victory, Japan has nuclear power energy as its strategic priority.

Banks as licensed and controlled as monetary policy by central banks or monetary authorities compete in oligopoly under similar set interest rates for deposits and loans. Financial crises and bank runs are strictly and authoritatively controlled or managed. These are to be totally avoided to the extent possible, but even Singapore was a "good house" in a bad neighbourhood in the 1997–8 Asian financial crisis because there were interbank linkages across the region. Only reputation and confidence matter with prudence and good banking principles.

In theory, barometric price leadership is where the "barometer" firm (not necessarily the dominant firm) is best to assess changes in market conditions to alter prices as followed by others. In the banking industry, the Development Bank of Singapore (DBS) as the largest bank is the barometer to set interest rates. In contrast, the Federal Reserve as the American central bank sets interest rates.

In many other oligopolistic businesses, they can be found in science and technology (S&T) as well as research and development (R&D) involving patents. Singapore's PUB NEWater as recycled water is one of the four taps mixed with water from reservoirs, imports from Johor and desalination. Before NEWater, in the 1990s, membrane technology as improved cost and performance is another source of drinkable water. As such, necessity is indeed the mother of invention for Singapore with five NEWater plants supplying up to 40% of its water needs, to rise to 55% by 2060. Singapore may be buying water from Johor at some historic agreement prices, but selling at high to home consumers is to induce saving water, not purely just to make profit.

Monopoly

This has a sole supplier or producer with good reasons for the resultant monopoly power. In economic theory, a natural monopoly is one where only one firm is sufficient or necessary to be the sole producers. This comes with economies of scale (see Chapter 2) as a monopoly suiting the market. Large-scale works best under a monopoly especially with a relatively small market on the demand side as consumers.

Splitting the small market into more producers as better competition for price and quality has the counter arguments of appreciable rises in unit costs of many producers rather than a monopoly catering to a small market as supporting its capital and operating costs. Making a practical case is for one national electricity company to produce and transmit electricity rather than a few lines, especially with reliance on imported oil, to deliver electricity to households and firms.

Economies of scale also enable specialisation as knowledge, know-how and experience grow and reside with the monopoly to pass lower resultant costs to consumers. This is the case for telecommunication and broadcasting by radio and television as well as mass entertainment among other reasons for news and broadcasting. These also necessitate government control of certain less desirable materials and information, from censorship to total ban of activities deemed as threatening national sovereignty.

In many other commercial cases, high sunk costs in capital, equipment, machinery, specialised manpower and such are being justified for a monopoly. For airlines, the reasons include the negotiation of air rights as aeroplanes fly into foreign countries with sovereign air rights. This makes airlines as monopoly state-owned enterprises (SOEs) as national carriers.

Singapore has used the terminology as government-linked companies (GLCs) as that sounds more politically acceptable especially when such GLCs go West to the US and Europe as linked rather than owned by the government. In practice GLCs are SOEs, as a matter of degrees, but they are more acceptable in Asia and ASEAN (Association of Southeast Asian Nations) where there are SOEs aplenty.

The same goes for ports with the requisite government regulations, licenses and statutes to protect marine territories (200 nautical miles beyond into the sea as sea-lanes). Crime as piracy in the high seas and other environmental concerns as protecting water and marine life fall under the ports with ships and vessels to regulate accordingly.

Think also of the European Union in constructing and running its Eurostar high-speed trains. The European Union (EU) operates as a single market and economy with even the euro as its currency. In similar thought, as and when the Belt-and-Road Initiative (BRI) from China materialises where high-speed trains run across around 70 sovereign countries, it is not just control of goods or passengers, with other health, environment and security considerations as challenges too.

In other areas, the need for similar control of certain factors of production as in uranium used for nuclear power generation as well as nefarious nuclear bombs come to mind. In other commercial settings, patents and copyrights matter, such as Polaroid having the patent for instant cameras.

As a monopoly lacks competition and deviates from all the positive features of competition to harm consumer welfare, monopoly as state or government monopoly seems to be justifiable with accompanying national political economy considerations. An optimum scale suiting a small market with one monopoly makes better sense as a state monopoly.

There are other redeeming features of a monopoly. First is supernormal monopoly profit can be as much managed as well as using them for upgrading economic performance in S&T and R&D pursuits. Such is the "price" borne by the monopoly for its market share to maintain its position. This and other considerations mean while profit-making is important as an objective for monopoly, other non-economic as political and social considerations matter too. In fact, the monopoly power has to be watched and regulated per the monopoly objectives.

In broader senses, state monopolies appear justified for public utilities from water to electricity. The HES dimensions are as relevant. Again, for Singapore when it started its defence industry by Singapore Technologies Industrial Corporation making armaments suited to Asian military. Such defence activities have high potential in S&T and R&D and they spin off other high-technology pursuits as knowledge-based. Overall, Singapore Inc. seems to work for the city-state.

Over time, as the private sector catches up to take over some of such SOE/GLC activities, with privatisation of GLCs. Indeed GLC privatisation as both passing over ownership to the private sector for its traditional advantages also means ample good listing in the stock market as another desirable outcome. Such privatisation offers more variety and choice for Singaporean savers with the CPF Investment Fund as another category for using CPF savings before retirement, in fact augmenting that.

Pricing strategies

Pricing rules for profit maximisation by the intersection of demand and supply curves hold as in Figure 3.2 as repeating Figure 1.6.

Also, the area above the price line and below the demand curve is the consumer surplus. The area below the price line and above the supply curve is the producer surplus. Thus, if price falls, the consumer surplus gains at the expense of loss of producer surplus; we know consumers love price falling. On the other hand, if price rises, the consumer surplus loses, but the producer surplus rises as price increases.

If the price change is due to a subsidy or a tax, the consumers gain or lose respectively. In practice, how elastic is demand is also of consideration. Simply put, if the tax is on a product the consumers still want despite the tax (tobacco, alcohol, car taxes), the producers can pass the tax burden over to consumers. The government achieves its policy aim as less of these three "sins", regardless of the consumers pay more for all three items with higher taxes; has this been accomplished?

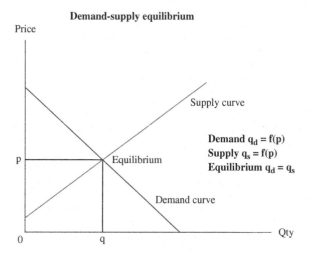

Figure 3.2   Demand-supply equilibrium for price and quantity

Other generic pricing strategies include marginal cost pricing (where MC = MR in theory, but in practice with indivisibility of inputs in many industries, the MC pricing strategy is unrealistic.

Another is incremental pricing concerning the relationship between large changes in revenue and costs rather than at the margin. Supply as affecting total revenue matters with changes in variable costs or incremental costs of producing an additional batch of the product.

Break even pricing sound right to match total cost with total revenue at that price, but in reality it is hard to identify such a break point, easier with a break area instead.

Mark-up pricing is similar to break even pricing except that it also incorporates a desired rate of pricing, also called cost-plus pricing.

A mix of factors other than price alone affect pricing strategies including

1. Product characteristics, with consumer perception as necessity, luxury, etc;
2. How well is the product distributed;
3. Market promotion as effective marketing, credit provision and advertisement;

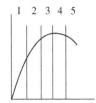

- 1 = introduction of product
- 2 = growth stage
- 3 = maturity
- 4 = saturation
- 5 = decline

Figure 3.3   Stages of life cycle and pricing

4. Product life cycle as in Figure 3.3 with different pricing strategies at the various five stages: high in initial stages to lower at the mature stage as competition has arisen, then saturation to falling off.

Pricing strategies work together with production costs as fixed costs remaining the same regardless of production, such as rents, fixtures, equipment and machinery as well as variable costs as raw materials, wages, electricity consumption and other utilities. Thus, while fixed costs are fixed and unchanged regardless of output, variable costs all rise with output rising.

Distinguishing further as short run and long run, short run has both fixed and variable costs while in the long run, there is only variable costs with no fixed costs. By definition, the long run is defined as no fixed costs, only variable costs. Over time, in long periods, firms also move from one scale of operations to another to mean a different set of cost relationships. New technologies, including going automated with robotisation for instance, to digital as in e-commerce, e-banking and such fixed and variable inputs change from more machines to less labour, especially unskilled labour.

Generally, across all four market structures, profit-maximisation holds. The PUB as a monopoly is as needed to negotiate the water agreement with the state of Johor, also for pricing to enhance the all-important water-saving habit of all users in Singapore. The usual commercial objectives of NEWater or Singapore Technologies Industrial Corporation also hold.

As a green city in a garden, rather than merely a garden-city with prolific tree-planting to beat global warming in an island with reclaimed land as fearful of rising tides as polar ice melts, Singapore is most mindful of HES dimensions. Electronic road-pricing (ERP) is as much to reduce traffic congestion by private vehicles as also for SMRT for economies of scale among other objectives. Thus, with rising oil prices, adjusting SMRT fares upward is with careful consideration of elder passengers among others.

Law of diminishing returns

The Law of Diminishing Returns in production holds in the short run, with both fixed cost (as machines) and variable costs (as labour). More and more labour employed to work with the same number of machines aims to increase output, which rises initially. Diminishing returns then sets in as more labour is not as effective, with the fixed factor unchanged.

In the long run, with only variable costs and no fixed costs, that is both labour and machines are variable, both can expand to increase output. Thus, with no diminishing returns, returns increases as output.

Returns to scale

In the long run, three possibilities in the relationship between inputs and output, are as returns to scale:

1. Increasing returns to scale for volume of output increasing more than volume of inputs;
2. Constant returns to scale for volume of output increasing in the same proportion as volume of inputs;
3. Decreasing returns to scale for volume of output increasing less than volume of inputs.

What are the examples of all three?

Economies of scale

Long run average cost curve (LRAC) is U-shaped, beginning with the falling arm due to increasing returns to scale or economies of scale with decreasing cost causing AC to fall. Then with constant returns to scale or constant cost production, it reaches a flat part to the lowest point on LRAC achieved as constant cost production. Finally, with continued increase of output, decreasing return to scale sets in with increasing cost production as LRAC rises. Economies of scale first falling to constant then rising to diseconomies of scale is illustrated in Figures 3.4 and 3.5.

Economies of scale can be internal as decisions and operations of individual firms as under their control as well as external at the industry level.

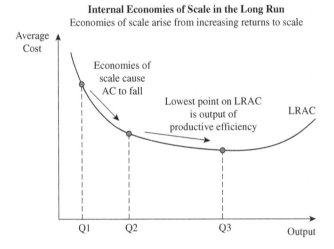

Figure 3.4   Long run average cost curve (LRAC)

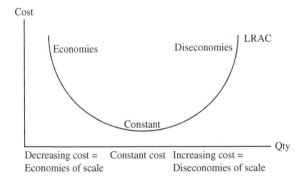

Figure 3.5   Economies of scale

Internal economies of scale include better use of labour and managerial skills as in large firms with division of labour and better career prospect as motivating staff. Investment of equipment increases in productivity as well as R&D. Procurement in bulk purchasing also lowers costs. Availability of finance and capital is positive. Diversification into different markets is strategic with promotion of different products as well as by products. Efficient transport and distribution also help.

External economies of scale occur at the industry level as associated with the industry growing over time, arising from available labour force for the industry with a concentration of suppliers specialising in ancillary firms in the locality as in supplying some components and inputs on an industry-wide scale. Infrastructure for the industry includes transport, housing, educational and medical facilities all enhancing labour productivity while lowering industry cost as a whole.

Competitive environment

Market structure from more competitive to monopoly affects the industry, which in turn affects prices and profits. More specifically, Michael Porter's five forces in a competitive environment make sense (Figure 3.6) as:

1. Power of buyers;
2. Power of input suppliers (for labour, raw materials, capital, etc);
3. Threat from potential new entrants into the industry;
4. Threat from substitutes;
5. Degree of competition or rivalry in the industry.

Over time, Porter's five forces or competitive environment also changes with

- Changing political environment (Trump's trade war with China since 2018);
- Changing economic environment (rise of China as the world's Factory, Japan as #3 in gross domestic product (GDP), digital economy);

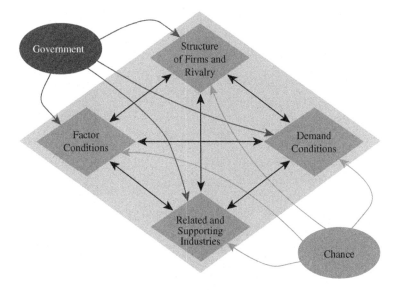

Figure 3.6   Porter's diamond of competitive advantage

* Changing social environment (ageing demographic);
* Changing technological environment (automation, robotisation, etc).

The acronym is PEST or STEP.

Applications

Think of the following situations to consider suggestions or responses to overcome the following challenges:

1. The Singapore Airlines (SIA) facing competition from other legacy airlines and low-cost budget airlines, started its own, Scoot, as cannibalising or complementary?
2. Traditional soap versus new body foam, foaming body wash, etc., is there competition?
3. More GLCs are privatised, e.g., can DBS be 100% privatised? Why, or why not?

Chapter 4

Consumer Theory

Introduction

This chapter considers households as consumers on the demand side as well as a factor of production as supply in the labour market, elaborated later in Chapter 5. Consumers as in market demand for goods and services further touches on types of goods as normal, inferior, Giffen and luxury with elasticities done in Chapter 1.

This chapter also looks into the effect of price change affecting consumer theory, as well as more on utility and the law of marginal utility.

Consumer theory

Consumer decisions comprise:

- What amounts of goods and services to demand for consumption?
- What amount of labour to supply in order to gain income for consumption?
- What to spend today, save for tomorrow as in saving as postponed consumption?

To a consumer, it is another basic see-saw or trade-off economic decision as in a fundamental equation:

Income earned by working = consumption + saving

In a 24-hour period, it seems to be divided into eight hours for working adults, eight as sleep and the remaining eight defined as leisure, but including time for transport to-and-fro work. Over time is beyond the eight-hour working time.

Disposable income (Yd income after tax) = consumption
+ saving (postponed consumption)

Apart from hours worked and income earned, other factors affecting consumer demand Qd is principally price, hence P = f (Qd). Other factors include prices of substitutes (coffee, tea) and complements (house, furniture, taste, advertising, credit (loans)), expectations of future price change and even government policy. Banned drugs as cigarettes are taxed to be costly to deter smoking as carcinogenic.

Consumption function

The consumption function for consumers is C = a + bYd with Yd as noted is disposable income as income after tax, with a constant as "a" in total C associated with tax and other aspects not available for consumption expenditure such as saving. The slope of the consumption in Figure 4.1 as "b" is the marginal propensity to consume.

It is any increment Δ in Yd as increment Δ to C. Logically, "m" as marginal propensity to consume and "s" as marginal propensity to save adds up to unity, that is

mpc + mps = 1

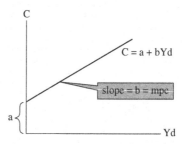

Figure 4.1   Consumption function

Consumers may choose to save to earn with bank interest to consume more later, or purchase big-ticket items as housing or holidays. Incidentally, housing is a joint household consumption in contrast to a cup of coffee.

While generally downward-sloping as in Figure 4.1, demand can be perfectly inelastic (vertical as in necessities as education and health services), perfectly elastic (horizontal, normal goods) or unitary elastics as a curve rather than a downward-sloping straight line. All things being equal, the flatter is the demand curve (smaller is slope b), the more elastic it is.

Utility

What is utility as consuming goods and services is for some satisfaction, as food or a vacation. Some satisfaction may be as a demonstration effect dubbed as keeping up with the neighbours (Jonses) as consumption due to peer pressure and unrelated to price as the driver of quantity demanded. This is clearly very subjective ranging from fashion to social status. Equally, what is consumer sovereignty as the ability to make consumption decisions is another question not subject to pure economics. Advertising plays on such influences.

Law of diminishing utility

Simply put, how many cups of coffee at one sitting to drink arises as after a certain number of cups, utility and satisfaction turn negative. This is the law of diminishing utility. As a consumer rule to spend on a myriad of goods and services with a limited budget, the ratio of marginal utility from the last dollar spent of each item to its price is the guiding principle:

$$Mux/Px = Muy/Py = Muz/Pz$$

An interesting poser is whether the law of diminishing utility applies to money. It does not seem to apply simply because money is what money does. We do not consume money as in coffee with diminishing utility. Money is a medium of exchange, enabling the consumption of many goods and services, thus no diminishing utility applies.

Indifference curve

Indifference curve is a device to represent preferences and used in choice theory. An indifference curve shows combinations of two goods for which a consumer is indifferent, that is, the consumer has no preference for one combination versus another. In Figure 4.2, bundles A or B render the same level of utility or satisfaction for the consumer.

For a given assumption on taste, a mapping of indifference curves for a given pair of goods is derived. Logically, indifference curves do not intersect, or contradictory or ambivalent preferences emerge. Distinct indifference curves are associated with different utility levels. The rational consumer prefers the higher, or right outermost, indifference curve as higher represents bigger combinations of goods providing higher utility levels.

If the goods are perfect complements, the indifference curves will be L-shaped. The best example of perfect complements comprises a pair of shoes, a left shoe and a right shoe. The consumer is no better off with several right shoes and only one left shoe. Additional right shoes have zero marginal utility without more left shoes. The marginal rate of substitution (MRS) is either zero or infinite.

The marginal rate of substitution on an indifference curve is the slope of the tangent at a point. It measures the opportunity cost. For food and clothing in Figure 4.2, MRS is the change in quantity of food to be given up for change in quantity of clothing ($\Delta y/\Delta x$). It is a negative ratio to depict a trade-off or opportunity cost, more of clothing at the expense of food and vice versa. In general:

$$MRS = - (\Delta y/\Delta x)$$

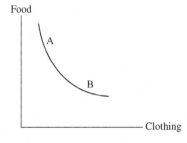

Figure 4.2   Indifference curve

Budget line

Consumers face a budget constraint as limited resources. The budget line (Figure 4.3) for a certain allowance depicts combinations of food and clothing possible. Total expenditure Y is the sum of what is spent on the two goods. Qy as derived is the budget equation where Y/Py is if the whole budget is spent on Y or the y-intercept and the slope is MRS = – (Px/Py). The consumer can choose any point on or below (sub-optimal) the budget constraint line:

$$Y = PxQx + PyQy$$
$$Qy = Y/Py - (Px/Py)Qx$$

Assuming constant prices and a fixed income in a two-good world, consumer equilibrium E in Figure 4.4 has the budget line tangent to the highest possible indifference curve. It maximises the amount spent on

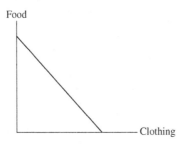

Figure 4.3   Budget line

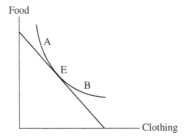

Figure 4.4   Consumer equilibrium

both goods together to equal the income of the consumer, and the indifference curve with the highest utility which is within the budget constraint. At tangency E, MRS is also the slope of the budget line or ratio of the prices of the two goods:

$$MRS = -(\Delta y/\Delta x) = -(Px/Py)$$

The equilibrium at E in Figure 4.4 may alter with price changes of either or both food and clothing as well as when the *ceteris paribus* assumption of a fixed income changes either way.

Price consumption curve

Suppose price of clothing falls to allow a larger amount purchased with the same clothing budget allocation. With food price unchanged, Figure 4.5 shows the change with the budget line pivoted on the y-axis, rotated outward to denote more clothing, enabling it to be tangent to a higher indifference curve. E moves to E′ with a larger combination of both food and clothing.

Tracing a series of price changes, a price consumption curve shown in Figure 4.5 is a locus of various equilibrium points. The price consumption curve reflects the law of demand as the lower the price of food, more food is consumed, or the inverse relationship between price and quantity demanded. In other words, the downward-sloping demand curve can be derived from the price consumption curve (Figure 4.5).

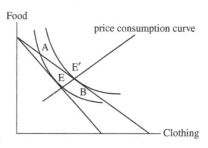

Figure 4.5   Price changes

Engel curve

Consumption changes when income changes. A higher income shifts the budget line outward and conversely when income falls. It is a parallel shift if prices remain constant. The outward shift of the budget enables a higher indifference curve to be attained as in Figure 4.6, from E to E″.

Repeated changes in income enable an income consumption curve, also called an Engel curve to be traced through E and E″. This is the relationship between the income level and consumption of a commodity. It is usually upward sloping to reflect more of the commodity consumed as income rises. This is true in general for normal goods as obeying the law of demand.

As a summary, Figure 4.7 shows derivation of a demand curve for food from price consumption curve and the Engel curve for food from income consumption curve.

Substitution effect and income effect

The effect of a price change can have a substitution and income effect in Figure 4.8 for normal and inferior goods. If price of coffee falls, the consumer may substitute tea for coffee giving rise to a substitution effect. On the other hand, as coffee is now cheaper, it is tantamount to a rise in income, as the consumer can afford more coffee by this income effect.

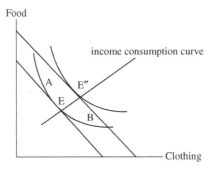

Figure 4.6   Income changes

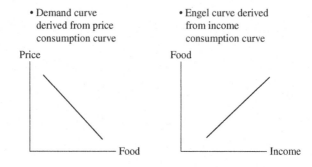

Figure 4.7   Demand curve and Engel curve

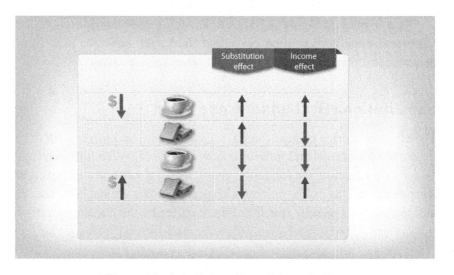

Figure 4.8   Substitution effect and income effect

Assuming rational consumer behaviour, the substitution effect of demand of a price change will always be opposite in direction to the price change. It becomes zero if no substitutions exist at all. The income effect, however, can either increase or decrease demand depending on the nature of the good as normal or not. The net effect depends on the relative strength of these two effects.

Substitution effect + income effect = net effect of price change

Consumer theory examines trade-offs and decisions consumers make as prices and incomes change. Decomposing a price change into a substitution effect and an income effect, the former price effect changes the slope of the budget constraint, but leaves the consumer on the same indifference curve.

The substitution effect will always cause the consumer to substitute away from the good which has become comparatively more expensive. For clothing and food as two basic needs, costlier clothing means less clothing. On the other hand, if the price of food falls, the price of clothing is relatively more expensive even if absolutely, it has not changed. The consumer may spend more on food, less on clothing, or food is substituted for clothing. Food and clothing may not be perfect substitutes, but some substitution is possible, up to a point.

Giffen and Veblen goods are two exceptions to the law of demand are. Strong inferior Giffen goods have both negative price and income effects. For potato as a Western staple with no substitutes, its stronger negative income effect outweighs its positive substitution effect. A price rise may lead to consumers cutting demand for meat to have more potatoes.

Salt is an inferior good, not obeying the law of demand. It has a single use for food taste, and households do not demand more or less salt with price change as it is a very low-priced item, consumed in small quantities. There is no substitute for salt, just demand price inelastic — no change in demand when price changes. It is also income inelastic — no change in demand when income changes. In fact, for health reason, less salt is better and sea salt is even superior.

A Veblen good has its demand increases as the price increases, because of its exclusive nature, appeal as a status symbol or quintessentially, a snob good of high-quality and coveted like diamonds. Both Giffen and Veblen, respectively luxury and inferior goods do not have easily available substitutes.

Types of good

A typology of goods in Table 4.1, from complements and substitutes to normal goods, luxuries and inferior goods emerge from consumption characteristics reflected in demand and elasticity. Elasticity is a

Table 4.1   Types of goods

Normal necessities	Normal luxuries	Inferior goods
Fresh vegetables	Organic vegetables	Frozen vegetables
Instant coffee	Fortified fruit juices, drinks	Water
Natural cheese	Luxury chocolate	Processed cheese
Shampoo, toothpaste	Antique furniture, art	Own brand, no brand bread
Retailed brands	Designer clothes	Second-hand, used goods
Rail travel	Chauffeured limousine, air travel	Bus travel
Public education	Private education	Home, self-education
Car, rail travel	International air travel	Seaside picnic

Table 4.2   Elasticity of goods

Type of goods	Price elasticity of demand	Income elasticity
Normal	Positive, elastic	Positive, elastic
Necessities	Inelastic	0 to +1
Inferior	Very inelastic	Negative
Luxuries	Very elastics, >1	Very elastics, >1

responsiveness of one variable to another, as also noted for the types of goods in Table 4.2.

Normal goods abide by the law of demand with an inverse relationship between price and quantity demanded. It has a positive income elasticity of demand; demand rises when income rises.

Within normal goods is a class of necessities. These are basic essential goods including food, clothing and shelter. Necessities have an income elasticity of demand of between 0 and +1. Demand rises with income, but less than proportionately owing to a limited need to consume additional quantities of necessities and as substitution to other goods occurs as real living standards rise.

Beyond a basic level, the demand for essentials like bread, toothpaste and newspapers is not very sensitive at all to fluctuations in income, or are income inelastic. In fact, to reflect a higher standard of living and quality of life, the consumer spends more additional income on non-necessities or luxuries.

Luxuries are commodities with an income elasticity of demand greater than unity, that is, very income elastic. Demand for luxuries rises more than proportionate to a change in income. Luxuries are items we can (and often do) manage to do without during periods of below average income and falling consumer confidence.

However, when incomes rise strongly as a stock market bonanza rally, consumers have the confidence to go ahead with big-ticket items of spending. Conversely in a recession or economic slowdown, luxuries as discretionary spending might be the first victims of frugality. Consumers tighten spending and rebuild saving and household financial balance sheets. Demand for luxury goods falls proportionately more than an income falls.

Many luxury goods also deserve the sobriquet of "positional goods" including Veblen goods. These are products where the consumer derives satisfaction (and utility) not just from consuming the good or service itself. Others may also see it as having the ability to afford such expensive commodities. Perversely, the higher the price of snub luxuries, the greater the snob appeal as in the diamond-water paradox.

At the other extreme are necessities as inferior goods. They may also not obey the law of demand with a negative income elasticity of demand. Demand falls as income rises relevant to staples (rice and bread substituted for finer food) and basic, low quality commodities (bus to private car). In a recession, the demand for inferior products might actually grow as living standards plummet, depending on the severity of income fall and income elasticity of demand.

The perception of a product may differ from consumer to consumer or across markets. A necessity to some might be a luxury to others. MacDonald may be cheap fast food to most, but a luxury in Moscow. Mobile phones pass from luxuries to necessities. The growing air travel market with rising income and technology is an example for segmented market and product development. Annual overseas holidays may be a luxury in the past. Lifestyle change as in Singapore as relatively high-income includes business-cum-vacation travel as more normal goods rather than luxuries.

For many products, the final income elasticity of demand might be close to zero, to imply a very weak link at best between fluctuations in income and spending decisions. In this case the "real income effect" arising from a fall in prices is likely to be relatively small. Most of the impact

Table 4.3   Substitutes and complements

Substitutes: coffee & tea	Coffee price up	Coffee demand falls	Tea demand up
Complements: coffee & sugar	Coffee price up	Coffee demand falls	Sugar demand falls

on demand following a change in price will be due to changes in the relative prices of substitute goods and services.

Substitutes or rivals are goods which can be used interchangeably or their demand affected by relative price and income changes. Cheaper prices lead to some substitution. Consumers substitute for cheaper goods with lower affordability as income falls. Goods used together are complements. Their demand goes up or down together as shown in Table 4.3. Higher (lower) prices of substitutes increase (reduce) quantity demanded. For complements, higher (lower) prices reduce (increase) quantity demanded. Independent goods are used on their own. An umbrella has few substitutes and no complements.

Factors determining market demand

The demand function is $Qd = f(P)$ where quantity demanded is a function of its own price, both endogenous variables. All other exogenous factors are held constant under *ceteris paribus*. Relaxing these constants including prices of substitutes and complements, income, tastes or preferences, population and demography as in a young or ageing structure, and government policies as encouraging or deterring certain consumption, shifts the demand curve accordingly.

Market demand

Market demand is a horizontal summation of individual demand at various prices as shown in Figure 4.9. The assumption of consumer sovereignty or consumer is king means individuals and households in aggregate may signal through quantity demanded, "invisible hand" or market-clearing price for supply equals demand.

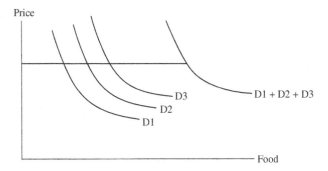

Figure 4.9 Individual to market demand

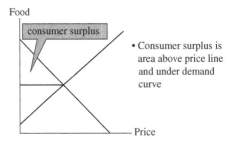

Figure 4.10 Consumer surplus

An excess demand raises price, signals to some consumers to lower demand as per the law of demand. Simultaneously, higher price through the law of supply increases supply which also helps to dampen price and satisfies the initial increase in demand. With both demand and supply at work, price may return to the initial equilibrium point. The converse works for excess supply.

In Figure 4.10, the area[1] denoting consumer is dependent on the shape (slope) of the demand curve. The more elastic is the demand curve (more substitutes), the larger the consumer surplus.

---

[1] Area of a triangle = half (base × height).

Chapter 5

Labour Market

Introduction

As noted in Figure 1.1 in Chapter 1, households as consumers (Chapter 4) are also inputs or a factor of production as workers in firms (Chapter 2). What goes around comes around from demand–supply or consumer–producer, respectively.

A labour market is non-physical with various ways of advertising for labour services or jobs specified by education, skills, experience, gender, age and other prerequisites as in Figure 5.1.

Demand for labour

Demand for labour by employers in the private and public sectors, at home and abroad comes from the suppliers or producers of goods and services. An interesting correlation between unemployment and inflation rates lies in the Phillips curve in Figure 5.2. The downward-sloping short-run Phillips curve implies a trade-off; lower unemployment at R has higher wage inflation at Q as a demand-pull effect is higher demand for labour, lower unemployment at higher cost.

Labour-intensive production may relocate to cheaper sources as firms migrate across the border from Singapore to Johor, Malaysia or Batam, Indonesia as desirable. Moving higher into more capital-intensive and skill-intensive industries means no more textile and garments, but to electronics including semi-conductors. Robotics and digitalisation in banks

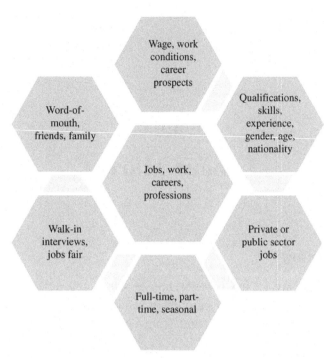

Figure 5.1   What, why, when, where, who, how to work

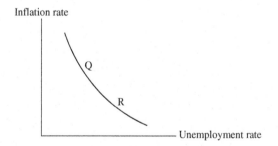

Figure 5.2   Phillips curve

switching to automated teller machines (ATMs), in turn replaced by mobile phones are further boosted by cashless payments from credit and debit cards to ez-link (prepaid) cards for public transport.

Unemployment

An understanding of the types of unemployment is to design appropriate labour policies to treat the causes more than the symptoms. In the long-run extreme, the Phillips curve becomes inelastic as vertical at N in Figure 5.3, having reached a natural rate of unemployment. Any increase in economic activity will be inflationary until more resources or higher productivity can dampen price increase.

A variation of the downward-sloping Phillips curve in Figure 5.3 as natural rate of unemployment at N with a vertical Phillips curve. The natural rate of unemployment is a sum of two types of unemployment:

- Frictional unemployment is always present when people change for better jobs, take time to look for desired jobs, as labour market information filters through.
- Structural unemployment is more common and increasingly more problematic as industrial changes lead to joblessness. The new economy demands a new set of skills as in information and communications technology (ICT). Globalisation is a double-edged sword; exacerbates job loss with relocations or business migration leaving a trail of high unemployment rate at home or enabling tapping global labour as for Singapore.

Figures 5.4 to 5.6 are in sight as the Report of the Committee on the Future Economy reflects the future is digital, with much to prepare,

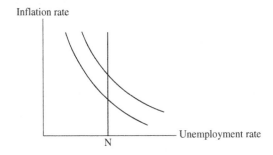

Figure 5.3   Natural rate of unemployment

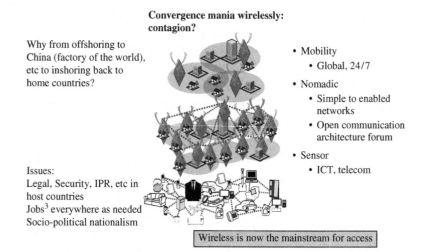

Figure 5.4   Industries, clusters, ICT = globalisation

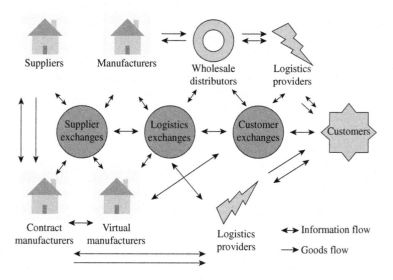

Figure 5.5   Global e-corporation network structure

including labour. Finding the right person for the right job involves a global talent search for a candidate who is skilled in 5G technology. Simultaneously, rewiring for rehiring responds to lowering structural unemployment of Singaporeans.

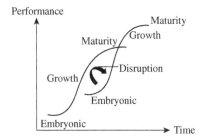

Figure 5.6   Double "S" disruptive technology curve

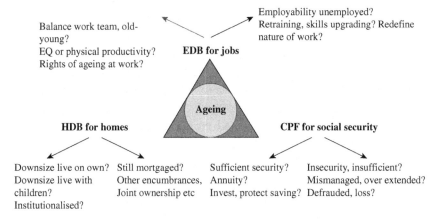

Balance work team, old-young?
EQ or physical productivity?
Rights of ageing at work?

EDB for jobs

Employability unemployed?
Retraining, skills upgrading? Redefine nature of work?

HDB for homes

Ageing

CPF for social security

Downsize live on own? Still mortgaged?   Sufficient security?   Insecurity, insufficient?
Downsize live with   Other encumbrances, Annuity?   Mismanaged, over extended?
children?   Joint ownership etc   Invest, protect saving? Defrauded, loss?
Institutionalised?

Figure 5.7   Iron triangle to ageing triangle

A greater policy concern is the iron triangle morphing to an ageing triangle as silver demographics after the postwar baby boom as illustrated in Figure 5.7.

Ageing Singapore as in Japan worsens structural unemployment as older workers may face problems in reskilling and retraining, lower wages in new jobs, other adjustments to work life with mismatch of acquired skills and rational expectations. Singapore has National Trades Union Congress (NTUC) and National Wage Council (NWC) as policy responses.

Other types of unemployment may not need as much policy concern like:

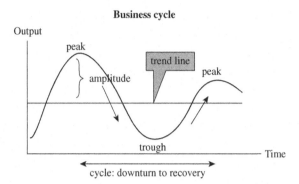

Figure 5.8   Business cycle affecting employment

- Disguised unemployment is peculiar especially in rural activities as more labour is "employed" than needed, due also to traditional social networks as in informal sectors involving families and friends and paradoxically, labour productivity is enhanced when such "excess" labour is removed and emplaced in industrial and urban sectors;
- Voluntary unemployment is a feature of skill mismatch or graduate unemployment with pay and career expectations to justify education and skills such that graduates do not take any available jobs;
- Seasonal unemployment is due to seasons and natural factors;
- Cyclical unemployment is due to business fluctuation (Figure 5.8) with macroeconomic policies as stabilisers.

Involuntary unemployment occurs in auctioned labour markets as indentured or tied by contracts as in the construction projects. Employability rather than unemployment is a tougher problem as those on the dole in Western welfare states resist rewiring for rehiring.

Elasticity of demand for labour

Applying the same formula in Chapter 1 for elasticity, price elasticity of demand for labour is negative to show the downward-sloping relationship between wage (price) and labour (quantity).

Inelastic for skilled labour   Elastic for unskilled labour

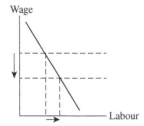 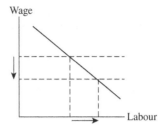

Figure 5.9   Elasticity of demand for labour

Elasticity of labour demand = – (% change in quantity demanded)/
(% change in price)

Figure 5.9 shows elasticity of demand for skilled labour as inelastic and elastic for unskilled. For the same fall in wages, demand unskilled labour increases more than skilled labour.

Supply of labour

In Figure 5.10, the population is either economically active (labour supply) comprising both employed and unemployed (remaining in the labour market, looking for jobs) plus economically inactive homemakers. Importing foreign labour is a policy choice for Singapore to top-up labour supply. Elsewhere, labour migration, aided and abetted by refugees as a new form of cross-border movement means each political system has ways and means to handle an appropriate labour supply policy. Salaries of employed maids enters the circular (Figure 1.1) as gross domestic product (GDP, Chapter 8), not proverbial unpaid housewives as mother, wife, sister or other relatives as naturally loving.

Minimum wage or workfare

It is a misconception that a minimum wage policy as socio-politically appealing will solve all labour problems if there are labour surplus and

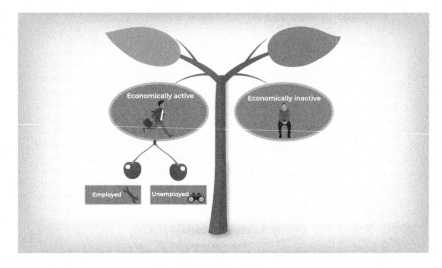

Figure 5.10   Population tree

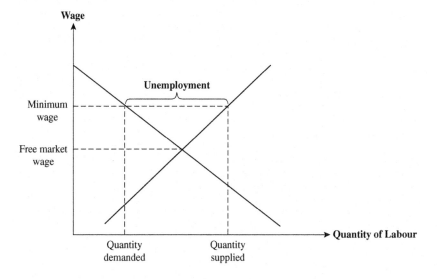

Figure 5.11   Minimum wage

high unemployment rates. Figure 5.11 shows minimum wage as a price floor, higher than free market wage. At best, a minimum wage is a tempo-rary measure to raise wage to improve labour conditions of poor developing countries. It is government intervention with intermittent calculations for sectoral and occupational wages across-the-board, not laissez-market as economically free and best.

A minimum wage policy treats the symptom of labour surplus, low-skilled and educated workers, hence low pay. Even over-populated countries have to treat these causes, not the symptoms. Legislated minimum wage is easy to make, difficult to remove. The government ends up with constant monitoring to adjust the mandated wage without market forces, productivity and global competitiveness as guides. Usually, trade unions in OECD (Organisation for Economic Co-operation Development) economies are the greatest advocates for sectoral and occupational minimum wages.

The International Labour Organization (ILO) first queried and suggested a minimum wage while the "official" reply was Singapore had good legislation under the Ministry of Labour (MoL) then ensuring labour supply and employment plus good industrial relations by NTUC followed by NWC in response to first oil crisis in 1973–4.

Since the last decade, Singapore has over 1 million low-wage foreign workers to augment, complement or substitute the local workforce. They work in a wide range of professions from lecturers and nurses to domestic and hospitality services and construction work; the latter deemed dirty, dangerous and demeaning or 3D jobs. Some Singaporeans are unable or reluctant to upgrade their skills in a timely manner.

Faced with a low wage trap with high cost of living leads to an academic debate of a minimum wage. However, it is not a minimum wage problem as a cure or protection. The labour surplus and unemployment in Figure 5.11 is simply unfit for aspirants of better-paid jobs who are unwilling to take low-paid and 3D (dirty, dangerous, demeaning) jobs. In fact, the problem with the minimum wage for Singapore is that it can cause unemployment of local workers as not rewired.

Singapore has two statutory boards in response. One is SkillsFuture under the Ministry of Education (MoE) to drive and coordinate the implementation of a culture and holistic system of lifelong learning. Right skills mastery and a strong ecosystem of quality education and training prepare Singapore to keep upgrading amid an ageing demography and a digitalising world as illustrated in Figure 5.12.

Emerging skill areas covered by SkillsFuture Series

Data analytics
National University
of Singapore

Cyber security
Temasek Polytechnic
and Singapore
University of
Technology and
Design

Finance
Singapore Management
University

Entrepreneurship
Ngee Ann
Polytechnic

Tech-enabled services
Republic Polytechnic
and the Singapore
University of Social
Sciences

Advanced manufacturing
Singapore
Polytechnic and
Nanyang
Technological
University

Digital media
Nanyang
Polytechnic

Urban solutions
Singapore Institute
of Technology and
Institute of Technical
Education

Source: SKILLSFUTURE SINGAPORE   SUNDAY TIMES GRAPHICS

Figure 5.12   Emerging skill areas covered by SkillsFuture Series

The other statutory board under the Ministry of Manpower (MoM) is Workforce Singapore (WSG) for employability and as a key social security pillar. Quintessentially, WSG oversees the transformation of local workers to avert the rewiring-rehiring-retiring trilemma and move them into the future digital economy.

Workfare rewards work and encourages up-skilling by supplementing the incomes and retirement savings of older lower-wage Singaporean workers, and providing funding support for their training. Workfare comprises two schemes as Workfare Income Supplement (WIS) and Workfare Training Support (WTS).

In line with Figure 5.7, WIS encourages eligible workers to work and build up their Central Provident Fund (CPF) savings for their retirement, housing and healthcare needs. They supplement their income and retirement savings through cash payments and CPF contributions.

Under WSG is P-Max, an adapt and grow initiative which aims to:

1) Help small and medium-sized enterprises (SMEs) to better recruit, train, manage and retain their newly-hired Professionals, Managers, Executives and Technicians (PMETs).
2) Enable SMEs to establish better communication channels between supervisors and staff and to adopt progressive human resource (HR) practices (e.g., goals setting, performance management) for newly-hired PMETs (Professionals, Managers, Executives and Technicians) within their SMEs.
3) Help newly-hired PMETs to better acclimatise to the new SME work environment and to encourage better retention of PMETs in SMEs.

Workfare is for both older lower-wage Singaporeans workers to self-train to up-skill and employers who send their older lower-wage workers for training. Instead of a minimum wage, Workfare is a form of wage subsidy correctly aimed to augment skills and pay for low-wage workers. Workfare is justified by the presence of a large pool of low-wage foreign workers as a better alternative to minimum wage.

Employers of low-paid foreign workers pay a foreign worker levy (FWL) which amounts to not a small sum in revenue, well utilised by the prudent government. The support Workfare over a minimum wage is rationalised in four reasons.

One is revenue from FWL is likely to continue exceeding expenditure on Workfare. While MoM does not publish figures on FWL revenue, it cited S$2.5 billion in Parliament.

Two is while a minimum wage can increase consumer expenditures as shown in studies for China and Germany, Singapore foreign workers are more likely to send remittances home than spend locally. As resource-deficient, totally open and reliant on imports from raw materials to consumer products, such leakages are massive. Both high marginal propensities to import and save combined with remittances of foreign workers are not negligible leakages.

Almost all countries with a minimum wage law also have unemployment benefits schemes.

Three is not surprising as minimum wage can cause retrenchment even on a voluntary basis. When unemployment benefits run out, the retrenched workers return to the workforce again. In policies, Singapore is historically against minimum wage and unemployment benefits. Its proven competitive advantage is in agility to up-skill and not rely on soft socio-political policies.

Finally, while there remains much to ponder in the new digital future in a fast-paced interconnected global world, Workfare remains the safest and proven policy with SkillsFuture Opportunities for training and retraining at all levels embrace individual empowerment as each citizen takes matters into his/her own hands and grabs every training opportunity for skills upgrade.

Substitution and income effects

Substitution and income effects of wage will change accordingly, with the net desirable effects. Negative substitution effects arise for work as economically active or economically inactive in Figure 5.11. Leisure still costs money.

The income effect needs to be distinguished at a low or high wage. Those earning high pay may be able to afford to not work, but leisure is not costless. The positive income effect is for low-wage earners, but negative for high-pay workers. Correspondingly, low-wage workers work more hours while high-pay workers opt for less hours, including over-time.

Labour force participation rate

As in Figure 5.11, defining labour force participation rate LFPR has:

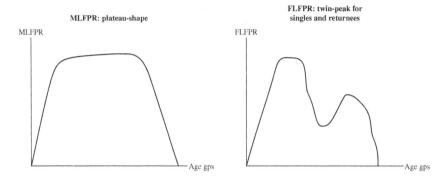

Figure 5.13 MLFPR and FLFPR

LFPR = (economically active / population) x 100%

The male labour force participation rate (MLFPR) is generally high and stays high until retirement or death. The female labour force participation rate (FLFPR) for young women of reproductive age is:

FLFPR = (economically active females aged 24–29/
population aged 24–29) × 100%

Typically, FLFPR for single females can be as high as MLFPR in Figure 5.13. With marriage and children, some females withdraw from the labour force to take care of families. If they return to work, a second peak in FLFPR in Figure 5.13, but still lower than the first peak. At a more mature age, higher family income as dual or even more by unmarried children in the same household is likely. Higher-earning female professionals can afford foreign domestic maids. Some rewiring may be needed as well for all as ICT and work norms are among some changes.

Productivity of labour

Productivity is the key in Singapore's labour market as labour-saving with capital-intensive production come with moving up to higher levels of industrialisation. Automation, mechanisation, robotisation and digitalisation are high-tech, substituting for low-skilled manual foreign workers.

Labour productivity as an input simply defined is:

Productivity of labour = output / labour input

For the economy as a whole:

Productivity of labour = Gross National Product (GNP)/
total number of hours worked

Total number of hours worked constitutes the labour force.

In an industry:

Productivity of labour = total output of industry / total output of industry

In a firm:

Productivity of labour = total output of firm / total output of firm

Productivity index is: productivity for a particular year / productivity
of the base year

Inherent difficulties in defining and measuring productivity include:

1) Numerator as output can be at various levels as national, industry, firm
   or individual.
2) It is easier to output across-the-board at the national level than for
   specific industry, firm or individual.
3) Where output cannot be divided or attributed to an individual (often
   necessary to determine reward/pay for effort), it is best to measure
   productivity at an aggregated average level.
4) Productivity of labour is hard to measure where output has an intangible component such as quality of work/service rendered.

Measurement of productivity is important for two reasons:

1) Productivity and real GNP
   Productivity of labour = real GNP / worker hours
   Real GNP = labour productivity x worker hours

2) Productivity and inflation
   Rapid productivity growth helps to limit the rate of inflation while slow productivity causes inflation to rise

Change in money wage (%)	– Change in productivity (%)	= Change in labour costs (%)
leads to	leads to	leads to
Nominal wage growth	Gains here help to offset increases in nominal wage growth, thereby help to restrain ULC	Unit labour cost (ULC)

As ULC changes are restrained, product price increases are restrained. This helps to boost competitiveness of products.

Formulation for open, import-dependent Singapore:

- Productivity gain restrains ULC growth, which limits product price increase to competitiveness.
- Productivities of both labour and capital matter as the inputs are used in combination to produce output.

Factors affecting productivity of labour include:

- Work attitude;
- Levels of skills (education & training (human resource development, HRD));
- Productivity management (resources and systems);
- Labour efficiency (manpower planning, human resource management, HRM), job enlargement;
- Entrepreneurship (risk-taking and creativity of business).

Factors affecting productivity of capital include:

- Machines (hardware) for mechanisation, automation, computerisation, robotisation, digitalisation;
- Technology (software inputs) including research and development (R&D), product technology, production technology and application engineering.

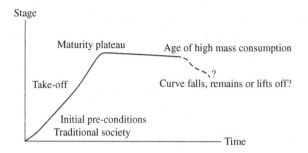

Figure 5.14   Rostow: 5 development stages

Productivity growth is not always on an upward trend. It is critical for Singapore to watch over time:

- Business cycles (Figure 5.8) affect both GNP growth and productivity growth.
- Small, open, import-dependent, resource-scarce mean many sources of leakages (high propensity to save (mps), high propensity to import (mps), reliance on foreign workers with remittances, exposure to regional and global financial crises among other contagious effects).
- A more mature economy where HRD and productivity growth may have reached their potential to focus on maintaining development (quality) rather than quantity (GNP), as in Figure 5.14.

The five stages of growth by Walt Rostow are:

1) Traditional society;
2) Pre-conditions;
3) Self-sustaining growth;
4) Take-off, drive to maturity;
5) Age of high mass consumption.

Quantitative growth (GNP) enables or is followed by qualitative growth as physical quality of life (PQLI) in terms of education, health and other aspects including clean air and water, even freedom, however defined.

Total factor productivity

Total factor productivity (TFP) with an accounting framework is:

GDP growth = employment growth + capital growth + TFP growth (k)

Defining total factor productivity as output per unit of combined inputs of labour and capital is the efficiency with labour and capital combined. It captures the tangible factors including technical progress to contribute to productivity. However, TFP is not directly as growth in GDP, labour and capital. The result is TFP measured as a residual (k).

Conceptually, TFP decomposed, comprising the following as policy tools:

1) Investment in human capital (HRD) in education and health;
2) Better management system (HRM);
3) Technological progress (capital investment, science and technology (S&T), R&D);
4) Economies of scale;
5) Improved labour–management (industrial) relations.

As a reminder, changing demography with ageing, low population reproduction rate among others have led to high reliance on imported labour, hence a foreign worker policy.

Roles of NWC, NTUC

Responding to imported inflation with the first oil crisis, the NWC was formed by the government in February 1972. It is a tripartite advisory body comprising the government, NTUC and Singapore Employers' Federation to make recommendations on wage adjustments. Prior to NWC's establishment, wage adjustments were negotiated by bargaining power by NTUC and management.

Apart from oil-induced inflation, the government was concerned that wage increases should keep in pace with national productivity gains as noted, otherwise higher costs of doing business also erode Singapore's competitiveness in the global economy. Careful tripartite deliberations make wage recommendations in line with long-term economic growth to ensure economic and social development.

The NWC meets annually to deliberate and forge national consensus on wage and wage-related matters. Based on the tripartite consensus, NWC guidelines reached during the deliberations are accepted and implemented. Singapore is thus investor-friendly, in contrast to more militant trade unionism elsewhere. Moreover, with NWC, NTUC and effective MoL/MoM legislation and enforcement, Singapore enjoys peaceful, harmonious relations. Full employment is the case as the high reliance on foreign labour is an indication. Employability rather than employment is the challenge with ageing and Industrial 4.0.

As noted, the traditional role of NTUC has thus morphed from traditional labour union functions for protection of workers, including wage, working conditions, safety among others to reskilling and up-skilling workers.

Starting as an institute with academic diplomas and degrees jointly awarded, NTUC LearningHub partners with SkillsFuture and WSG. It jointly offers a place-and-train arrangement, its Professional Conversion Programme for ICT sector (ICT PCP) to train mid-career switchers to become qualified Infocomm Technology professionals.

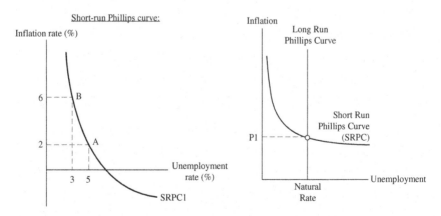

Figure 5.15   Phillips curve

Singapore is in an enviable position with low inflation and low unemployment or of no trade-off between inflation and unemployment as depicted in the Phillips curve in Figure 5.15. Maintaining a harmonious balance for its local and foreign workers may be more challenging and complex.

Chapter 6

Government

Introduction

The same political party in government focussing on economic growth and development with a more visible than invisible laissez-faire hand of a free market economy seems to work as successfully with good leadership. Over time, socio-political factors may be more dominant with economics as income and employment are settled.

The Committee on the Future Economy (CFE) in 2017 for digitalisation has private sector representations and inputs, with the government pivotal in guiding and ultimately implementing the plan. It has seven strategies as:

1) Deepen and diversify our international connections;
2) Acquire and utilise deep skills;
3) Strengthen enterprise capabilities to innovate and scale up;
4) Build strong digital capabilities;
5) Develop a vibrant and connected city of opportunity;
6) Develop and implement Industry Transformation Maps (ITMs);
7) Partner each other to enable innovation and growth.

It has identified six clusters comprising 23 sectors involving a whole-of-government approach with various statutory boards as coordinating agencies. For example, under modern services comprising professional services, ICT and media as well as financial services, the

Economic Development Board (EDB), Ministry of Information and Communication (MCI) and Monetary Authority of Singapore (MAS) are in charge.

Nature of public and private goods

The economic role of government stems from the distinction between public goods and private goods (goods including services) in Table 6.1. A category as merit goods falls within public goods like education and health desirous and necessary for all citizens. They can be mixed goods as produced by both government and private sector as public schools and hospitals.

Commodities produced/supplied and consumed/demanded in a market are pure private goods as opposed to public goods. Private goods as priced and sold in the market may exclude those unable to pay, thus divisible and rivalrous in nature in Table 6.1.

Public goods as part of public expenditure, financed by tax revenue are also available for non-taxpayers as a society as a whole. Public goods in government intervention are justified for two reasons, economic and welfare. Economic market failure stems from two characteristics of pure public goods:

- Non-rivalrous in consumption where consumption by one individual does not deprive another's consumption, in turn owed to the second feature, namely,
- Joint consumption as in defence, police or justice which are consumed jointly by all once these public goods are produced by the government.

Table 6.1   Characteristics of public and private goods

Public goods, e.g., defence, police	Private goods, e.g., hamburgers
Jointly consumed	Divisible
Non-rivalrous	Rivalrous
Free ridership	Excludable by price
Government produces or provides	Private sector produces

Table 6.2   Mixed good as matrix of rivalry in consumption

Consumption	Rivalrous	Non-rivalrous
Joint	Mixed good (jammed public road)	Pure public good (defence)
Non-joint	Pure private good (pizza)	Mixed good (postal service)

A mixed good is defined as when only one of the two characteristics holds. It can be rivalrous and joint in consumption, or non-rivalrous and not jointly consumed. It may be privatised over time. All examples are provided in the following matrix in Table 6.2.

Role of government

From public–private goods as distinguished, government agencies and government-owned and operated enterprises produce public goods. They are provided via government financing with the private sector which is more efficient as producers.

The welfare justification for the government to produce or provide selected private goods and services like education, health care, housing and public transport is due to externality. A third party enjoys positive externality, by the society as a whole when individuals consume these social services. Better education, health and housing are both basic human rights and means of income distribution and social mobility.

Unlike private goods where consumers pay the cost for the benefit internalised, public or social goods with externalities have external benefits as subsidised. The subsidy acts as a social cost or price for the social benefit of better education or health benefiting the economy as a whole.

Similarly, negative externality is involved as in the consumption of cigarettes or production of polluted air, water and noise by factories. The government may deter such consumption or production via a tax. The revenue pays for the social cost of negative externality as in public health and environmental protection.

State philosophy, level of economic development and maturity of markets decide how much welfare versus self-determination by individuals and markets suit best. A pure capitalist market system based on incentives and profits may be economically efficient, but not equitably desirable in income distribution and welfare. A pure socialist system promises equity in welfare without an incentive structure for productivity and relative performance. A mixed economic system combines the two in shades of grey.

State-owned enterprises (SOEs) or government-linked companies (GLCs) operate on private sector principles, some profit-making and some public objectives like all GLCs of Temasek Holdings, a sovereign wealth fund (SWF) with some government ownership as in the Development Bank of Singapore (DBS). But DBS functions as a commercial bank. Privatisation of SOEs or GLCs is by listing on the stock for market participation as shareholders.

Rather than an ideological divide between state and market, a public–private partnership (PPP) is relevant and useful in most state-market economies. The laissez-faire market is suited for private goods while the government has its functions in supplying public or social goods, even mixed goods with the externality argument. Income distribution and equity in a welfare-conscious economy may emplace the government's role over and above economic functions.

The government has a wide-ranging discretionary role as much as automatic in-built stabilisation as with the market mechanism. This is more so when there are external forces of supply and demand, international trade and financial markets to manage. Such exogenous factors are beyond the control of individual economies.

The government's participation in regional (Association of Southeast Asian Nations, ASEAN) and international bodies such as World Trade Organization (WTO) and International Monetary Fund (IMF) to facilitate some coordinated influence and action on regional and global matters. Environmental protection for pollution of air and water or safety in all aspects, land, air and sea is as much to protect these territorial and sovereignty rights as these are international public goods.

Government intervention also occurs in goods with a strong externality as in merit goods. Externality effect means others enjoy the government production or provision in education and health. These are also distinctively meritorious for all citizens to enjoy good education and health, also enabling them as good workers. Equally, goods like pollution with negative externalities fall under the government's care.

In the final analysis, the role of the government is to ensure three macroeconomic objectives:

1) Full employment;
2) Price stability, no inflation or deflation; and
3) An optimum and desirable rate of growth.

Chapter 6 covers (1) and (2). The CFE in 2017 also projects economic growth and development for the next five to 10 years.
The government is equipped with two sets of tools as:

1) Fiscal policy;
2) Monetary policy.

Fiscal policy

Fiscal policy is in taxation, expenditure and public debt. The government imposes taxes with a taxation policy to generate revenue for government expenditure on public goods and some consideration on income distribution as well. Three bases for taxation in Figure 6.1 also define types of taxes.

Both individual/personal income tax and corporate/company tax are most widely used to generate the bulk of tax revenue. For Singapore, the government has been reducing income tax, especially corporate tax to match Hong Kong's rate to be competitive in attracting foreign companies and investors. To make-up for revenue loss, it introduced the goods and services tax (GST) with GST rate being increased over the years. However, while individual income tax is progressive as in Figure 6.2, both corporate and GST rates are flat as the same rate for all as regressive.

Approaches and principles to taxation individuals with resulting impact are in Figure 6.2.

Some taxes are direct as income tax levied on and paid by the tax-payer concerned. In contrast, indirect taxes include GST imposed and shifted between consumers and buyers. as consumption-based. A sales or value-added tax (VAT) may seem to fall on sellers who can shift the tax burden somewhat by pricing tactics. Consideration is not to ignore any inflationary impact for such consumption-based taxes.

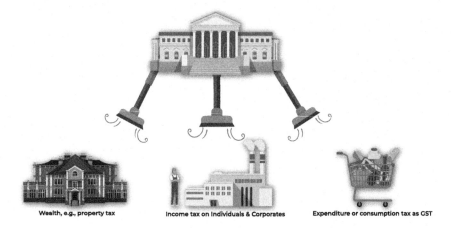

Figure 6.1   Tax bases as types of taxes

Approaches	Impact
• Ability to pay eg income tax • Benefit-based earmarked taxes, revenue finesse benefits, eg tourist cess for expenditure on tourist industry, infrastructure	• Progressive income tax, rich pays more as income distribution • Proportional all pay same amount • Regressive, poor pays more as benefits more

Figure 6.2   Taxation principles

Another feature of taxation is avoidance of double taxation when individuals and companies pay tax twice, to the host governments where they work and reside as well as to home governments. One of them, usually the home government would agree to forgo taxation as accepting tax paid to host countries. Such double taxation agreements (DTAs) help promote foreign investment and trade as beneficial countries over time.

Wealth-based taxes include property tax, estate duty and land tax. High vehicle taxes including Singapore's certificate of entitlement (COE) may be to restrict car ownership for traffic control, but affects foreign company cars as well.

Base of taxation:	Income
	Consumption/Expenditure
	Wealth
Approach/Principle:	Ability-to-pay
	Benefit
Typology/Classification:	Direct eg income, property
	Indirect eg GST, VAT
Impact:	Progressive
	Regressive
	Proportional

Figure 6.3 Summary of tax bases, principles and impact

Figure 6.3 summarises of tax bases, principles and impact.

Monetary policy and role of money

Monetary policy is on money enabling exchange beyond barter trade. The functions of money and its role in a monetised economy with banks and financial intermediaries, follow the quantity theory of money.

Money has a number of functions:

- Unit of account to enumerate the myriad of economic activities in an economy.
- Medium of exchange so the assumption of double coincidence of wants in barter trade is relaxed. Money as payment enables specialisation and division of labour as money represents purchasing power.
- Store of value which can appreciate or depreciate over time.
- Standard of deferred payment which allows loans and interest rate to finance economic activities. Loans allow risk-taking and entrepreneurs with ideas, but not finance.

People hold money for transactionary (same as medium of exchange), precautionary or speculative purposes. Interest rate matters only in determining the demand for speculative aim. Cash is held when interest rates on bank deposits or equity returns are low.

The following definitions of money supply go from the narrowest, most liquid to broader, less liquid monetary aggregates. How effective is monetary policy depends on how interest-elastic are the various components of money:

- Notes and coins or money in circulation as the narrowest definition of M1.
- M2 = M1 + demand deposits + travellers' checks.
- M3 = M2 + fixed deposits + certificates of deposit (CDs).
- M4 ... as other forms of money as near money or *fiat* money are included (stocks and shares, assets as in property and real estate, etc).

Money supply is controlled by the central bank in its role to issue currency and affect liquidity through credit expansion or credit destruction. A distinction is made between note issue based on balance of payments (BoP) reserves which guarantees the value of a currency and money printing without such backing. Printing money is inflationary deficit-financing.

Money supply is not changed by note-issue, but by credit expansion or credit destruction which is dependent on a money multiplier. This is determined by the central bank's setting of a statutory reserve requirement when deposits are placed in banks. The money multiplier for credit expansion is:

Money multiplier = reciprocal of statutory reserve requirement

A 10% statutory reserve requirement implies every $100 deposited in a bank enables the bank to lend out $90 as loans and keeps $10 with the central bank. The statutory reserve requirement is an important monetary policy tool.

Using the multiplier, every $100 allows a total credit expansion of 10 × $100 or $1,000 with a multiplier of 1/10. A higher statutory reserve requirement tightens up liquidity, such as 20% or 1/20 for a multiplier of 5. This generates credit expansion of $500 instead of 10 for $1,000.

Credit destruction works the other way around, when a withdrawal is made instead of a withdrawal. Banks lose deposits, so credit is "destroyed" in contrast to created.

Central bank

The central bank at the apex of a financial system has the following roles:

- Note issue as liquidity for gross domestic product (GDP) growth.
- Manages monetary policy and exchange rate policy.
- Ensures discipline via a prudential supervisory role for banks and all deposit-taking financial institutions including insurance companies and pension funds.
- Develops money market (local, foreign currencies), capital market (short-term equity, stock and shares, and long-term bonds), overall financial development.
- Government banker and financial advisor, manages the public debt.
- Lender-of-last-resort as the banker to all banks, when liquidity, not solubility, is the problem to prevent any disruptive systemic run-on-the banks.

In theory, note issue is based on BoP reserves which backs up money issued and affects the exchange rate. If BoP reserves are high to support a given money supply, the currency strengthens and vice versa. In reality, the exchange rate policy depends on a fixed or floating regime. The central bank intervenes or lets market forces work, respectively.

Also in theory, a central bank is autonomous and independent from the government or a separation of monetary policy from fiscal policy. This separation is to ensure the government cannot resort to deficit financing through note issue. Ideally, with close cooperation, the central bank and government ministry should coordinate monetary policy and fiscal policy in unison.

A bank as a firm basically trades in money. It makes a profit from differential interest rates. It accepts deposits from surplus households to lend to deficit households and firms as investment and for expansion. Islamic banking views interest as usury or *haram*, redefines *riba* to be Sharia-compliant, not just capital waiting as return on time.

The difference between liquidity and solubility lies in a non-performing loan (NPLs), defined as not serviced by the lender/debtor for three months and more. A bank makes market-based decisions on what and to whom it lends with due diligence on credit worthiness using the central bank's credit bureau. Financial crisis as in the Asia 1997 crisis is due to irrational exuberance, excess liquidity, unwise extended credit and NPLs.

The central bank as MAS (Monetary Authority of Singapore) in Singapore has to manage high liquidity and inflation with limited tools. The underdeveloped financial market limits saving and investment instruments to efficiently absorb and recycle funds in the circular flow. Classic herd instincts, market sentiments and exuberance pushed the bullish then bearish stock market run by the first quarter in 2006. Initial public offers (IPOs) mandated at a fixed Dh1 price and banks flouting the central bank's 1:5 credit rule for IPOs, are contributory factors.

Quantity theory of money

The theory can be succinctly stated by referring to the infamous "equation of exchange":

$$MV = PT$$

where M is money supply, V its velocity, P the price level and T the level of transactions.

Three pillars are implicit in the quantity theory of money:

- V and T are fixed with respect to the money supply.
- The supply of money is exogenous.
- The direction of causation runs from left (MV) to right (PT).

With V and T fixed and M is exogenous, then an increase in the supply of money will lead to an exactly proportionate increase in the price level. Thus, money supply expansions only cause price inflation. To the Monetarist school of thought, inflation is everywhere a money matter.

Keynesian economists differ somewhat. Supply of commodities is given by the "real side" of the economy. Say's Law, in particular says that supply creates its own demand or supply is accompanied by the demand for commodities. Money is demanded as a liquidity preference, required for transaction, precaution and speculation.

Rewriting the equation of exchange:

$$M/P = T/V$$

where T/V is now the demand for money necessary to fulfill the transactions T, given the institutional constraint V.

Because output is given by the real side and the demand for money is an institutional arrangement, then V and T are more or less fixed. The only variables which remain, then, are M and P. If the equation above holds at all times, then if M rises, we necessarily need P to rise by the same amount. This is the restatement of the quantity theory.

If M increases and T/V are fixed, then M/P > T/V, that is, money supply is greater than money demand. People get rid of their excess supply of money by demanding more of every good, thus the prices of all goods rise, that is, P rises, until this extra demand is siphoned off. The real value of money supply is brought back down to the level of real money demand (T/V) and equilibrium returns once again.

This Monetarist explanation, then, provides a theoretical rationale for the left-side causation: money supply increases will be met by an exactly proportionate increase in prices. This needs a stable T/V or a stable demand function for money, couched in terms of transactions demand. Indeed, the Monetarists or Monetarism is dedicated precisely to establishing this stable relationship empirically.

Government expenditure policy

Governments raise tax revenue to spend on public goods, especially on public infrastructure, even subsidised housing as HDB (Housing and Development Board) flats in Singapore. Figure 6.4 shows two government expenditure funds. Ministries make estimates of revenue (tax and non-tax as from sales of land and investment) and expenditure.

The Minister for Finance presents the consolidated government budget and statements to parliament for debate before passing into legislation for implementation. At the end of the fiscal year, the government has to explain any under- or over-spending as checks-and-balance and validation.

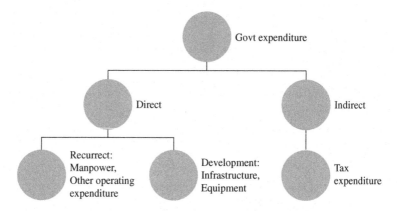

Figure 6.4   Classification of government expenditure

Government intervention and consequences

With the roles of the government as clear and legitimate, government intervention occurs even in laissez-faire market economies. The division between public–private stands to reason for some intervention. All government intervention with stated benefits and any foreseeable consequences are inevitable.

Income distribution is as necessary as low incomes as poverty exists with the high- and middle-income groups. How much to subsidise to promote a high degree of a welfare state is a political economy choice. The elected government with by its election promises re-judged as delivered or otherwise. The process is political as well.

Exchange rate policy

Figure 6.5 shows the difference between fixed and flexible exchange rates. Fixed or pegged to the dollar at a chosen historic rate, it is maintained by central bank intervention whenever demand for the dirham changes.

A supply of currency kept for exchange rate intervention incurs an opportunity cost. The trade-off is a stable exchange rate is favoured for a trading economy. The other alternative of a free market floating exchange

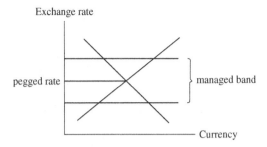

Figure 6.5   Fixed versus floating exchange rate

rate obviates central bank intervention, but suffers volatility. A mix of these two extremes is a managed float with intervention only when the pre-determined band is breached.

Many Asian economies hit during the 1997/8 financial crisis broadened their bands to accommodate speculative volatility on their currencies. As the crisis involved NPLs and bank defaults, crisis economies were hard pushed by retaliatory depreciation to maintain export competitiveness. But it led to speculators who expect a return to pegged rate. Band widening makes it harder for speculation as long as central banks have the official reserves to stand by the band.

The economic and political implications of a delinking or depegging from the US dollar constitute a separate matter. Most economies peg their currencies to the dollar simply because the US is usually their largest trading partner and/or investor. A basket of currencies weighted by trade pattern and partners may even out exchange rate volatility.

Monetary policy works on money supply, interest rate and other financial regulations as functions of the central bank. Historically in Singapore, the Board of Commissioners of Currency issued money supply before the MAS taking over to function fully as a central bank without any change in name.

Given Singapore with a highly open economy based on international trade and investments, in practice, the MAS executes a monetary-exchange rate policy. It is neither a fixed exchange rate nor a free, flexible exchange rate policy, but a managed float shown in Figure 6.6.

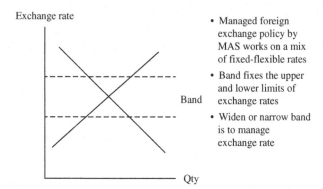

Exchange rate

- Managed foreign exchange policy by MAS works on a mix of fixed-flexible rates
- Band fixes the upper and lower limits of exchange rates
- Widen or narrow band is to manage exchange rate

Band

Qty

Figure 6.6   Managed floating exchange rate policy

Generally, Singapore enjoys an overall BoP from both its current account (goods and services) and capital and financial account. Strong reserves result which technically supports a strong Singapore dollar. However, a strong dollar hurts exports while it benefits imports. Given Singapore's high dependence on imports, the latter feature as a strong dollar is good for imports, leaves using other policies to help exporters.

Exporters benefit from market promotion tax write-offs and other spending as human resource development as tax deductible. The MAS does not resort to manipulating the exchange rate as "cheating" and can be subject to trade disputes and arbitration in the WTO.

Incomes policy

Incomes policy is a collective governmental effort to control the incomes of labour and capital, usually by limiting increases in wages and prices. Such policies directed at the control of inflation, may also indicate efforts to alter the distribution of income among workers, industries, locations, or occupational groups.

As seen in Chapter 5 on labour market, Singapore does not strictly have an incomes policy, but with National Wages Council (NWC)'s recommendations and ways and means including finessing rewiring and retraining, incomes are affected even if indirectly. Countries with highly centralised methods of setting wages tend to have the greatest degree of public or collective regulation of wage and price levels.

Public sector reform

Chapter 5 also shows public sector (government and GLCs) reforms in the labour market to meet the challenges of Industry 4.0 and prepare Singapore for the future digital economy.

Privatisation of GLCs in Singapore is part of government reform. It is not necessarily the government withdrawing or diminishing its role. It means a relook to keep up to relevant in government roles and functions. Thus, Singapore needed GLCs in early formative years until the private sector grows and matures and is ready for privatisation to take over. The government may have other GLCs and roles with changes over time. Generally, a larger and effective market private sector is better than a big government as predatory.

Simply put, the government takes care of macroeconomic policies (Chapter 8) while the free market involves production theory (Chapter 2) and consumer theory (Chapter 4). There is no fixed rule or formula for division as socio-politics stages of growth and development are as diverse.

Chapter 7

International Economy

Introduction

In this chapter, we first examine why nations trade, that is why international trade as noted by by Adam Smith, expanded by David Ricardo to trade based on competitiveness (revisiting Michael Porter's diamond in Chapter 3). The gains from trade are clear; less clear is how to protect infant industry.

International trade involves exchange rates as affecting prices of imports and exports, captured in the current and capital accounts of balance of payments (BoP) with equilibrium and disequilibrium to consider. The US–China trade war by President Donald Trump is classical as politics possibly superseding economics.

The trade environment with economic integration as in ASEAN FTA (Association of Southeast Asian Nations Free Trade Agreement) to EMU (European Economic and Monetary Union) needs clarification as the EU (European Union) faces Brexit. Finally, Singapore as a small, open and global economy, has trade as its lifeline, especially trade in services.

Theories of trade

Figure 7.1 serves as an opening to international trade via globalisation. It is like six blind men trying to figure out different parts of the elephant as different economies in trade.

What is Globalisation?
Why Financial Globalisation?

Figure 7.1 What is globalisation and international trade?

Source: Manfred B. Steger, Globalization: A Very Short Introduction (Oxford: Oxford University Press, 2003).

Globalisation like international trade is a mix of politics, culture, environment, economics, religion, ideology among many other dimensions. Does international trade involving different trade partners also feel like different parts of the same elephant with varying emphasis in international trade for economics or politics? Trump's trade war with China is a good example with trade inevitably also touching on culture, environment, religion and ideology.

Adam Smith touted absolute advantage as a basis for trade, as a country being more productive for traded goods based on absolute resources rather than comparative advantage as the relative productivity of countries in trade.

Assuming that Malaysia has absolute advantage in palm oil, Thailand in rice for their specialisation and trade as mutually advantageous for both. Specialisation and trade advantage in both countries based on laissez-faire, free market with policy of minimum government interference works best in theory. Malaysia and Thailand trade in exchanging palm oil and rice.

Following the law of comparative advantage, Malaysia specialises in and exports palm oil (smaller absolute *dis*advantage than rice) or has comparative advantage in palm oil, to import rice from Thailand. Laissez-faire still holds, gains from trade need not be equal, but trade is based on comparative advantage (relative), not absolute advantages.

The reality is the political economy of trade, more politics (all domestic) than economics. Michael Porter advances competitive advantage as policy-induced in contrast to what absolute and comparative advantages have in terms of resources endowed by nature. Singapore as resource-deficit is a good follower of Porter's five forces (see Figure 3.5) with policies to induce its competitiveness in trade, especially in services.

Static gains from trade mean more production and consumption as both countries specialise with gains. Dynamic gains from trade involve transfer of technology, skills, expertise, cross-border collaborations among others, as expanded by David Ricardo to trade based on competitiveness (revisiting Porter's diamond (Figure 3.5)).

Gains from trade, protection of infant industry

For both Malaysia and Thailand, moving from their primary agro-based sectors into their secondary sector, turning raw materials into finished manufactured products as higher value added are as relevant for modern international trade. Both have also gone into their tertiary sector as trade in services; Malaysia into banking services and Thailand into tourism services.

The infant industry argument in manufacturing is similar to mothers caring and protecting infants until they reach a more mature age to feed and clothe themselves. Infant industry as both new and entering into foreign markets cannot compete easily abroad is protected by import tariff or quota shown in Figure 7.2. The results include less import, rise in domestic output, government revenue from import duty and a deadweight loss that nobody gains.

While arguable to justify infant industry or any other protection with subsidies, they should all graduate as competitive with a suitable timetable. Retaliation from others as tit-for-tat can go on indefinitely. Protection once given is hard to remove, especially with nationalistic and political sentiments. It is hard work and unpopular to move to competitive strategic policies.

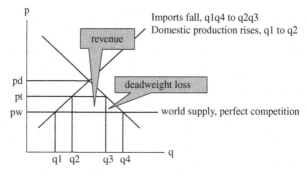

Tariff or quota have same effects, with import quota
calibrated to equal tariff

Figure 7.2   Import tariff or quota

The US–China trade war started by President Trump in 2018 based on unfair trade practices by China including enforced transfer of intellectual property. Instead of improving its comparative and competitive advantages to rebalance its trade deficit, "make America great again" is Trump's political solution. China rising peacefully may understand, but still China retaliates with its own tariffs on US imports.

Non-tariff barriers (NTBs) for protection have grown, including technical, administrative and other regulations based on health standards, for instance. Cases of voluntary export restraint (VER) may be like Japan agreeing to export less cars to the US as a gesture. Export subsidies and dumping are challengeable as unfair practices, as cartels like Organization of the Petroleum Exporting Countries (OPEC) too.

Dumping excess products as exports with low prices may attract a countervailing duty (CVD) or anti-dumping duty from the other side. It is a long and arduous process to detect and prove dumping as unfair trade. Going to WTO as dispute settlement arbitration is as tedious and costly.

International exchange rates

International trade involves exchange rates as the price of one currency relative to another with a stable rate of exchange corresponding to foreign reserves in balance of payments supporting such relative prices.

Two systems determine exchange rates, as fixed exchange rate (examples in Hong Kong and Gulf Cooperation Council (GCC)) and flexible or floating exchange rate (Singapore, around a band) in Figures 7.3 and 7.4. In practice, depreciation and appreciation artificially change exchange rates to cure trade imbalances. Countries accused of unfair manipulation of exchange rates potentially face retaliation.

It is noteworthy that with international trade, the US dollar also serves traditionally as an international currency with bullion gold and oil among other commodities prices in US dollar, also a currency of choice given the US as the largest economy and its political stature. With Asian trade, use

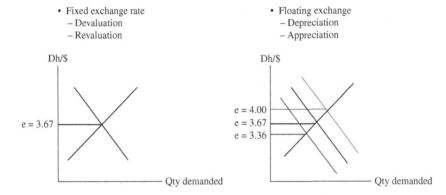

Figure 7.3   Exchange regimes

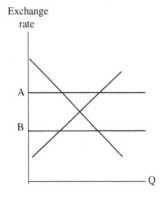

- S$ floats within an undisclosed band AB set by MAS
- MAS widens or narrows band to change exchange rate of S$ as relative prices of exports and imports
- Strong S$ may hurt exports, but helps imports
- Help exporters by other ways eg support HRD, overseas marketing trips, other capital expenditure
- Small, open Spore is totally import-dependent, to watch import prices as crucial

Figure 7.4   Floating exchange rate within a band

of the Japanese yen also yielded a yen bloc, the same with EU and its euro within the euro zone. The rise of China, by 2019 replacing Japan as the second largest economy by gross domestic product (GDP) now raises the quad of currencies in international trade as ¥€$ to ¥€$R adding the renminbi.

Factually, US suffers from its BoP deficit vis-à-vis China's BoP surplus with corresponding official reserves to back up their respective currencies. Si in God we trust as printed in the US dollar or in China to trust with its largesse?

Balance of payments

Balance of payments (BoP) records all external trade (exports and imports) activities under the current account and capital financial movements under the capital accounts. Together, the current and capital accounts as surplus or deficit accrues in reserve assets, adding to the official reserves. In Figure 7.5, for Quarter 2 in 2019, exports of goods and services for Singapore (S$216,651 million) as exceeding imports of the same (S$184,659 million) together with primary and secondary income balances yield a current account balance of S$21,497 million for a small, resource-deficient economy. Together with its capital and financial account balance of S$53,513 million), its accumulated official foreign reserves is a healthy S$272,239 million to back-up its dollar.

Current account captures merchandise trade, service trade and unrequited transfers or unilateral flows of goods and services as gifts or transfers from abroad without payment as for traded goods and services.

Current Account Balance	21,497.40
Exports of Goods and Services	216,651.70
Imports of Goods and Services	184,659.40
Primary Income Balance	-8,144.70
Secondary Income Balance	-2,350.20
Capital and Financial Account Balance	53,513.20
Reserve Assets	-32,021.50
Official Foreign Reserves	272,239.30

Figure 7.5   Singapore balance of payments, Q2 2019, S$m

Singapore has moved away from its traditional deficit in current account to earn a surplus as in Figure 7.5.

The capital account has items induced or affected by policies as in attracting direct foreign investment (DFI) as one form of capital flow with a large surplus in Figure 7.5. This is strategic for both the actual DFI accompanying the multinational companies (MNCs) to transfer skills and technology for Singapore's constant upgrading.

Aggregating items in the current and capital accounts in Figure 7.5 gives the overall BoP as generally doing quite well for a small open, resource-lacking city-state. Its policy-induced competitiveness as well implemented from the planning stage works effectively with a whole-of-government approach.

$$\text{BoP} = \text{current account} + \text{capital account}$$
$$+ \text{balancing items (errors and omissions)}$$

Errors and omissions arise with trade documents for imports/exports to be as officially accurate and not illegal as in smuggling and other nefarious activities. All BoP surplus adds to official reserves kept in foreign currencies and assets with reserves at the International Monetary Fund (IMF) to back up the Singapore dollar. An elected president since 1993 guards the official reserves as the "second key" besides the Parliament. This is the national net-egg for all Singaporeans.

Economic integration

Figure 7.6 shows trade liberalisation by tariffs and NTBs and the five steps to economic integration. First, a country itself removes its tariffs unilaterally. Next two countries liberalise trade by removing tariffs together as bilateral as in a free trade agreement (FTA). For ASEAN, it has a separate FTA on goods (ASEAN Trade in Goods Agreement, ATIGA) and another on services (ASEAN Framework Agreement on Services, AFAS).

From bilateral FTAs, the next as customs union further liberalises movement with a common external tariff as in Figure 7.7. Moving further, a single market adds factor and asset (labour and capital) mobility, then to

Trade liberalisation: tariff, NTBs

- Unilateral (national)

- FTA (bilateral)

- Regional (RTA, ASEAN, EU)
  - Preferential trading area
    step-by-step cuts tariff
  - Free trade area (AFTA)
  - Customs union
  - Single market
  - Monetary union (€zone)

- Multilateral (WTO)
  - GTA/WTO consistent
  - MFN, market access,
    national treatment

Figure 7.6 Trade liberalisation and economic integration

	No Internal Trade Barriers	Common External Tariff	Factor and Asset Mobility	Common Currency	Common Economic Policy
Free Trade Area	×				
Customs Union	×	×			
Single Market	×	×	×		
Monetary Union	×	×	×	×	
Economic Union	×	×	×	×	×

Figure 7.7 Different stages of economic integration

a common currency as the euro for the European Economic and Monetary Union (EMU). The final stage is an economic union with common economic policy.

The Asia Pacific Noodle Bowl

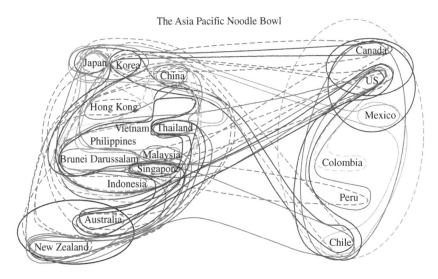

Figure 7.8   Spaghetti bowl effect of FTAs in Asia

Clearly, EU with some 28 sovereign governments (before Brexit) has politics in the way. Its final integration as EMU is without political integration. Only the US has both economic and political integration of 50 states and a single currency, US dollar. More FTAs as spaghetti bowl effect in Figure 7.8 mean many FTAs, different sets of rules all entangled, ends not meeting each other.

Singapore as a trading nation

As a small open economy without resources, Singapore has implemented its policies as a whole-of-government as in Figure 7.9 as an iron triangle of jobs–housing–social security. The Economic Development Board (EDB) creates jobs, the Housing and Development Board (HDB) for public housing and the Central Provident Fund (CPF) for retirement. Ageing in Figure 7.10 adds employability as a new challenge.

Figure 7.11 summarises the acute challenge in Singapore's manufacturing cluster with the EDB and Figure 7.12 illustrates the diversifying into manufacturing-related services.

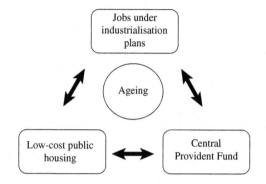

Figure 7.9   Triangle of jobs–housing–social security

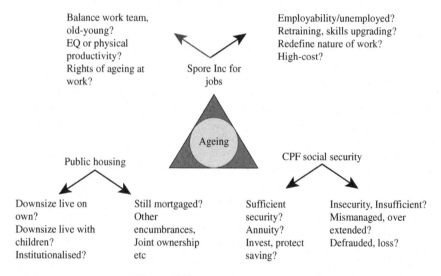

Figure 7.10   Iron triangle to ageing

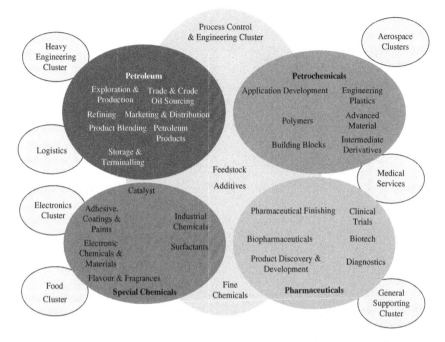

Figure 7.11 Singapore manufacturing clusters, not produce a drop of oil

A knowledge-based economy in Figure 7.13 with value-adding pursuit in Figure 7.14 results in a smiling face, positive outcome all round.

The smiley value-added curve in Figures 7.14 and 7.15 is a conceptual model of the shift to a globally integrated manufacturing-cum-services economy.

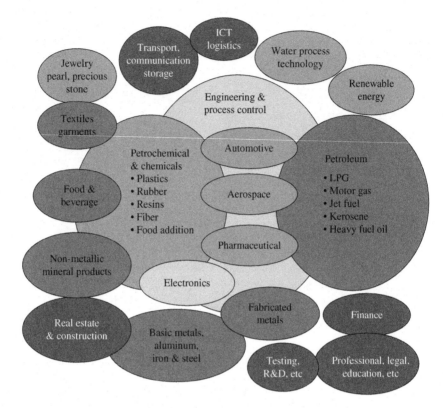

Figure 7.12   Singapore Industrial Cluster: Manufacturing and Services

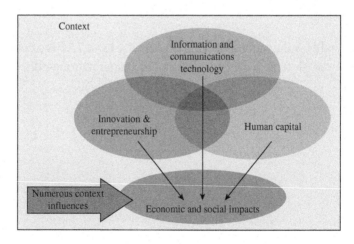

Figure 7.13   Knowledge-based economy

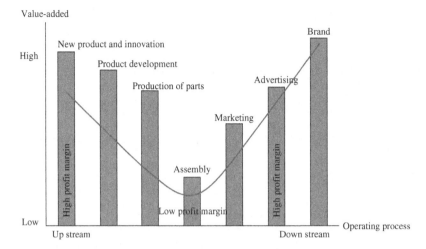

Figure 7.14   Value-added smiling curve

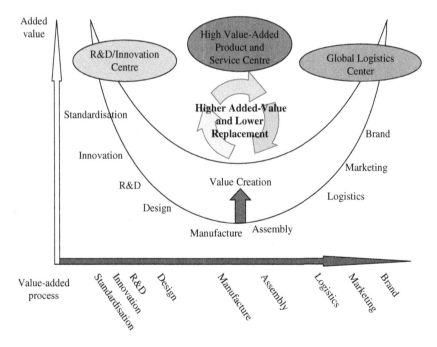

Figure 7.15   "Smiley Face": Conceptual model of the shift to a high value-added, globally integrated, services economy

The recommended videos demonstrate how world events have been shaped by international economy forces:

GFC Explained	https://www.youtube.com/watch?v=Q-zp5Mb7FV0
Global Financial and Monetary Systems in 2030	https://www.youtube.com/watch?v=Xrno41ToLl8
Euro Crisis Explained	https://www.youtube.com/watch?v=ttuXQWV_dtQ

Chapter 8

Macroeconomics

Introduction

This chapter begins by explaining gross domestic product (GDP) to gross national product (GNP). Other items include inflation, especially imported inflation for Singapore and the index of misery. On the determinants of national income, items include aggregate demand and aggregate supply to result in macroeconomic disequilibria and policy options for Singapore.

GDP to GNP

Figure 8.1 shows the circular flow of income with:

1) Market for goods and services involving firms and households (as both consumers and workers); and
2) Market for factors of production (land, labour and capital).

The circular process is through demand and supply by both markets (goods, services and factors) and actors involved (firms and households). Gross domestic product (GDP) measures all output as total value of goods and services produced within the territorial limits of a country, over a period of usually one year. In other words, Figure 8.1 is for all markets, producers (firms) and consumers (households) in one country (e.g., Singapore).

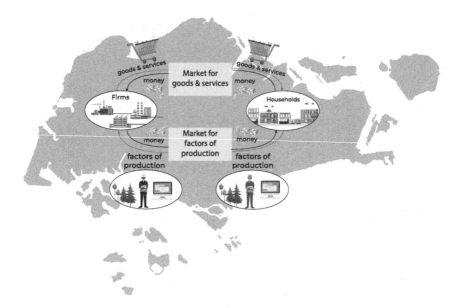

Figure 8.1   Circular flow of income

With international trade (Chapter 7), markets, producers (firms) and consumers (households) are also from the rest-of-the-world (ROW), noting Singapore as one of the most open economies to depend on trade and ROW. Gross national product (GNP is GDP plus factor income (both goods and services as well as factors of production)) which is more relevant for Singapore's case.

GNP = GDP + factor payment accruing to nationals from abroad
      − factor payment owing to non-nationals

GNP = GDP + net factor payment from abroad

If factor payment accruing to nationals from abroad exceeds factor payment owing to non-nationals, net factors payment is positive; negative as the converse. Both GDP and GNP concepts are correct as suiting the economy. Singapore as small and open, with as high a dependence on imports and exports, GDP is measured. By definition, GDP is subject to domestic monetary and fiscal policies for macroeconomic stabilisation while GNP is relatively outside of Singapore's control as such with greater external volatility. Both GDP and GNP statistics compiled serve as checks-and-balances as well.

Prices are relevant for a distinction between nominal GDP and real GDP over time, that is, with a GDP deflator to yield real GDP:

$$\text{Nominal GDP} / \text{real GDP} = \text{GDP deflator}$$

As a qualitative measure or as quality of life or standard of living, GDP per capita is GDP / population. Such quality measurements also have other indicators including consumer price index (CPI) as inflation.

Three ways of measuring GDP (or GNP) are as follows for an open economy with international trade:

1) As sum of final expenditures used universally:

$$\text{GDP} = C + I + G + X - M$$

2) As sum of total factor income (from land, labour and capital):

$$\text{GDP} = \text{wages} + \text{profit} + \text{rental} + \text{interest}$$

3) As sum of value-added created in each economic sector where value-added is defined as output less inputs:

$$\text{GDP} = \text{sum of (gross output} - \text{total material input)}$$

Inflation, imported inflation

Inflation occurs when the average level of prices for a basket of goods and services rises. With oil prices rising, inflation is a global concern rather than the reverse as deflation as less of a phenomenon. Price indices measure inflation; the most common is the consumer price index (CPI) based on a typical consumer basket of goods and services.

Over time, both adjustments take care of changing composition of the consumer basket of goods and services from:

- Changing consumption patterns, as demographic from young to ageing, other lifestyle changes;
- New products, obsolete ones;
- Quality changes.

Types of inflation include:

- On demand side: demand-pull inflation as during festivals as for Christmas gifts;
- On supply side: cost-push inflation as OPEC (Organization of the Petroleum Exporting Countries) oil prices causing wage price spiral;
- Imported inflation (for Singapore).

Inflation has both costs and benefits, with costs as:

- Real income costs of inflation resulting in fall in living standards for fixed nominal income recipients;
- Information destroyed by inflationary conditions with speculation, uncertainty and even profiteering (hoarding of basic necessities, too) as high;
- Distortionary costs result with inefficient decision-making in both consumption and production. For example, people may have committed enormous obligations for housing monthly mortgage payments, then find them unaffordable in inflationary times. This means to buy now before housing prices become unaffordable with inflation, as real estate prices escalate. The purchase is also desired as investment too.

Benefits are:

- A little inflation provides incentives needed for changes to relative prices;
- Capital accumulation and growth;
- Check/ease expanding government spending relative to private spending via an inflation tax.

Index of misery

This as a new index in the US and EU measures how misery is caused by both high inflation and unemployment; a sum of both twin-evils as inflation rate and unemployment rate possibly offering some trade-off in policy. With stagflation (GDP stagnant amidst inflation as OPEC high oil prices as the cause), such a trade-off occurs as renewable energy is discovered to lessen inflationary imported oil prices with added green industries and jobs in commensurate.

Determinants of national income

Two traditional schools of thought hold in the determination of national income:

1) Classical school assumes full employment and the "invisible hand" of the price mechanism as perfectly competitively in allocating resources under a perfect market structure.
2) Keynesian economics (arising in the 1930s during the Great Depression, from trade wars by US and Europe then) identified the lack of effective demand as the cause of downturns and recessions as cyclical. Unlike Classical assumptions of full employment and flexible prices, as well as reliance of the private sector, Keynesian theory is more on government spending, with G to counteract C and I as ineffective.

Aggregate demand (AD) and aggregate supply (AS)

In theory, AD = AS defined respectively as:

- AD is defined as total output demanded at alternative price-levels in a given time period, holding all other things constant (*ceteris paribus*).
- AS is defined as total output supplied by producers as willing and able to supply at alternative price-levels in a given time period, holding all other things constant (*ceteris paribus*).

Macroeconomic disequilibria

In theory, the intersection of AD and AS provides the equilibrium price level and quantities as demand and supply. In reality, supply shocks occur in OPEC price rising or other natural catastrophes including climate change affecting crops and meat supplies. The resulting disequilibria, especially in the short-run include:

- Unemployment where excess supply of labour is retrenched;
- Inflation when there is excess demand for goods and services.

Policy options

Macroeconomic stabilisation policies have the government in action through G to achieve equilibrium including by:

- Shifting AD curve;
- Shifting AS curve called supply-side economics;
- Do nothing to allow the economy to re-equilibrate itself through market forces of demand and supply.

The government has various tools to re-equilibrate as needed:

- Monetary policy using money supply-interest rate to affect the level of output. Generally in a recession, an expansionary policy calls for increasing money supply. In an inflationary (boom, heated) situation, a contractionary policy by reducing money supply cools inflation and the overheated economy.
- Fiscal policy employs tax and expenditure measures to either contract or boost the economy in an overheated or underperforming initial condition.
- With monetary and fiscal policies, supply-side economics also calls for deregulatory measures to encourage supply (in recession) or discourage it (boom).
- Exchange rate policies may further work as a high Singapore dollar is used to fight imported inflation.

- Other trade policy options, like switching to alternative sources of imports for Singapore may work for certain supplies from inflationary sources to less-inflationary supply; sometimes with some persuasion on demand as switching from Thai rice to rice from Bangladesh.

Chapter 9

Geoeconomics and Geopolitics

Introduction

First, the premise is geoeconomics and geopolitics go hand-in-hand like two sides of the same coin. However, unlike a coin, geoeconomics and geopolitics do not work as two halves or have economics and politics as neatly distributed in practice. They are likely to act in simultaneous tenacity as necessary vis-à-vis any perceived rival.

Witness the trade war started in 2018 as President Donald Trump used the economics of "unfair" trade by Americans buying more from China dubbed the Factory of the World. It is not Chinese buying more from the US as balance of payments (BOP) shows, thus deemed "unfair" trade. There is no trade theory behind the trade war, only sheer politics for Trump's re-election for his second presidential term. President Xi Jinping is fully cognisant of this to keep his predecessor Deng Xiaoping's promise of China rising peacefully. After all, President Xi as life-long president in China has time on his side.

This chapter reminds all of 21st-century globalisation (see Figure 7.1 on globalisation), information and communications technology (ICT), digital economy, including financial technology (fintech) and block chain. With Singapore's Committee on the Future Economy (CFE), the new digital economy also involves a sharing economy and circular cities.

Geoeconomics and geopolitics

Two indicators in Table 9.1 and Figure 9.1 show the rankings of global competitiveness and projected gross domestic product (GDP), respectively. As seen in Table 9.1, Singapore has overtaken the US as top ranked country in the 2019 Global Competitiveness Index 4.0 by the World Economic Forum. Figure 9.1 reports that by 2060 China will overtake the US by GDP (see https://asia.nikkei.com/Economy/US-and-China-to-fight-for-top-GDP-in-2060-while-Japan-dips-to-5th, 1 August 2019) while Japan will fall to 5th place after India and Germany.

On Singapore, the CFE convened in January 2016 to develop economic strategies for the next decade. In its report published in 2017, over 9,000 stakeholders, including trade associations and chambers (TACs), public agencies, unions, companies, executives, workers, academics, educators and students were consulted in the process. The CFE has built on the 2010 Report of the Economic Strategies Committee (ESC), taking into account both significant structural shifts in the world in global growth, global productivity growth, global value chains as all changing, with Singapore in response to both threats and opportunities.

The CFE for a digital Singapore economy follows the digital age and technology as in the US and China in the lead, among others. President Trump's trade war for "making America great again" is to sharpen its

Table 9.1   2019 Global Competitiveness Index 4.0

Singapore	84.8
US	83.7
Hong Kong SAR	83.1
Netherlands	82.4
Japan	82.3
Germany	81.8
Sweden	81.2
UK	81.2
Denmark	81.2

Source: World Economic Forum

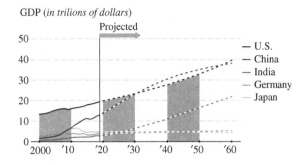

Figure 9.1 Projected GDP to 2060

Source: Governments, Japan Center for Economic Research (projections)

stance of keeping "America First" with an expected more adversarial stand against China. As China displaced Japan as the largest economy in the world by GDP in 2011, the global order in Figure 9.1 is not as pleasing to the US to begin with.

Digital technology as the key to business as already mastered and led by US and Chinese information technology companies to monopolise the world rankings of market capitalisation is a race. While the US is the leader of the digital economy and sharpening its "America First" stance accordingly, China is no mean rival. Japan struggles with stalled productivity in addition to a shrinking and ageing population, and may even lose its position by GDP as third, to trail the US, China, India and Germany in Figure 9.1.

Lessons from ageing Japan may be illumination as probably only India and Africa are still demographically youthful. Three factors identified for Japan's dismal long-term forecast in Figure 9.1 are first, intangible assets will become more important than tangibles, such as plants and equipment as the basis for wealth creation. Intangible assets are not physical but produce value-added to include software, intellectual property rights (IPR) and operational or organisational know-how.

The second factor is data sharing mechanisms needed for enhancing productivity which unlike general goods, data as non-rival in nature, can be used by many simultaneously to generate multiple spillover effects. For example, plotting the movement of people by examining electricity consumption data enables shops and restaurants to streamline their purchasing and staffing more accurately to predict customer visits.

The third factor is unsurprisingly as in Singapore, the importance of maintaining an open global economy. Globalisation results and is here to stay, but also needs specialisation to improve productivity by fostering competition and information exchange. More cross-border services become increasingly available thanks to digitalisation, with e-commerce, e-banking among others to be imperative not to impede the free flow of data.

China in 21st-century globalisation, ICT, digital economy, fintech and blockchain

In a word, China arriving to be leading in the new economy rather than traditional US or any European state is in evidence. In March 2019, the French President Emmanuel Macron invited his counterpart Angela Merkel to Paris to meet President Xi on his state visit. Subsequently, both Merkel and British Prime Minister Theresa May separately met Xi in Beijing in September 2019. All seems as curious and enchanted as Marco Polo's epic journey and stay in China around the 13th century. The rest is history.

China today is atop ICT, digital economy, fintech and blockchain with the likes of Tencent, Alipay among others. Chinese visitors also top all over with Chinatown streets in Singapore bearing names in Hanyu Pinyin. From Factory of the World, China will turn into Consumer of the World from travel to everything else, no least in education and health services in demand.

Singapore in ASEAN (Association of Southeast Asian Nations) does matter to China as ASEAN supplies raw materials from rubber, tin and palm oil to the Factory of the World. Singapore's airport and seaport as ASEAN hubs matter as well.

Singapore's CFE and its Greater Southern Waterfront (GSW)

First, the CFE Report in 2016 is in one word, digital. Its six strategies encompass

1) Deepen and diversify international connections;
2) Acquire and utilise deep skills;
3) Strengthen enterprise capabilities to innovate and scale up;
4) Build strong digital capabilities;
5) Develop a vibrant and connected city of opportunity;
6) Develop and implement Industry Transformation Maps (ITMs);
7) Partner each other to enable innovation and growth.

In all, China is a needed and viable partner as almost nearest and dearest. That said, simplified Mandarin with Hanyu Pinyin chosen by Lee Kuan Yew over traditional Mandarin as used in Hong Kong and Taiwan must prove itself as Chinese to China's interests. Politely or otherwise told by China, Singapore is a non-claimant in the Spratly Islands dispute that should refrain from interfering or learn from Philippine President Rodrigo Duterte in wooing China with potential handsome results. Duterte's fifth visit in three years to China in 2019 is in contrast to him not making a single trip to the US as Filipino president.

Apart from its CFE ambitions, Singapore is making history in relocating its port in the southern part of the city-state to Tuas as shown in Figure 9.2.

As the construction of the Greater Southern Waterfront gets underway, the Port of Singapore Authority (PSA) port terminals will be moved to Tuas by 2027. The port relocation is due to Tuas' proximity to Jurong, an industrial district. In addition, Pasir Panjang Terminal will be shifted by 2040, freeing up prime land for re-development. It will be an opportunity to reshape the GSW into a new place to live, work and play. Prime Minister Lee Hsien Loong gave the details in his National Day Rally Speech in 2019 (see https://twitter.com/hashtag/ndrsg?src=hash&lang=en).

The GSW will provide homes for living, business areas and recreation spots for locals and tourists. Even Sentosa's Merlion will be demolished as Sentosa-Brani Master Plan reshapes the two islands with a multi-sensory walkway — Sentosa Sensoryscape. The comprehensive blueprint to redevelop Sentosa and Pulau Brani includes game-changing leisure, tourism destination plans for new spaces, concepts, rejuvenated beaches. The Sentosa Development Corporation (SDC) will implement the master plan in phases for the next two to three decades, with construction for the

Figure 9.2   Greater Southern Waterfront

first milestone project — a multi-sensory walkway — to be commenced in the fourth quarter of 2019 and completed in 2022.

Singapore has to keep reinventing itself as much to impress China too as Singapore's Building and Construction Authority (BCA) sees potential for construction hardware and software activities in China's Belt and Road Initiative (BRI). The efficiency and turnaround time achieved in Changi Airport and PSA Port speak for themselves and as brand names China would need for its BRI across some 70 countries all the way to the UK–Europe.

An explanation on the BRI can be viewed in the following video: What is the Belt and Road initiative? https://www.youtube.com/watch?v=ACbbz0rOv6A

Conclusion

Small, open economy (SOE) with state-owned enterprises (SOE) called government-linked companies (GLCs) as SOE^2 being ruled by bureaucrats is as formulaic for Singapore, in contrast to equally small and open Hong Kong as China's Special Administrative Region (SAR) which is run by tycoons. The CFE has taken into account global and regional geoeconomics and geopolitics to plan significant global structural shifts impacting on Singapore's SOE^2.

As global growth is subdued as much by the US–China trade war as ageing demographics all round, global productivity growth has yet to catch up with technology and digital impetus. As long as the next Global Financial Crisis (GFC) is not originated from China, and the US, Europe, maybe Japan too continue to have innovative companies and people to work with, Asia is a growing continent with ASEAN as emerging markets.

For Singapore to navigate through the new economy, both hands need to clap with Singapore workers needing to catch up in basic economics and policy-makers employing their economic thinking. Singapore companies and its labour movement are as poised with rewiring, rehiring and not retiring, to tap into several growth sectors. The millennial generation is ICT and digitally equipped, though a bit short in history to know and value the past as relationships matter.

The rise of the middle class and urbanisation in Asia will work well to Singapore's advantage, but the latter needs to be humble and skilful to sell its wares and services. The gap between Japan and ASEAN is no less and although Singapore is advanced by OECD standards, the city-state still wants to be deemed developing, like its ASEAN neighbours.

Health, environment and security or safety (HES) form a standard and branding for Singapore. That is acceptable as a global standard with Singapore offering finance, hub services, logistics, and all urban solutions. Clearly, staying at home for work is not an option as the millennial workers need to venture out, especially into parts of Asia like ASEAN and China.

Printed in the United States
By Bookmasters